· T R O P H I E S ·

Library Books Collection
Collection
Teacher's Guide
Grade 5

Orlando   Boston   Dallas   Chicago   San Diego

Visit *The Learning Site!*
www.harcourtschool.com

Printed in the United States of America

ISBN 0-15-326185-4

8 9 10   71 010 09 08 07 06

Contents

Using Trade Books

> *"Children's exposure to and enjoyment of good quality literature has long been recognized as key to building positive attitudes about reading. Sharing stories, informational books, and poetry with children has become increasingly valued for its cognitive contribution to children's literacy development."*
> — Dorothy S. Strickland

Literature in the Classroom

Guiding students to become effective, enthusiastic readers is a major goal for every teacher. Research confirms the experiences of many teachers who have found that creating a classroom environment that surrounds students with language in every form is an important step in achieving this goal. Students need to hear, read, and use both formal and informal language for a variety of purposes and in a variety of formats and settings.

A key ingredient in enriching students' experience with language is providing quality literature for them to read, discuss, and explore. The wider the selection of available reading materials, the more likely it is that a student will come upon that one special book that sparks a new interest, expands a horizon, or produces a significant insight. The discovery of a particular subject, author, genre, or style often motivates students to seek out similar works on their own and to share their enthusiasm, which may well be contagious, with classmates. Successful and rewarding reading experiences lead to increased motivation and a lifelong love of reading.

Using trade books, either in conjunction with *Trophies* or in other ways, is an excellent method for exposing students to a wide variety of fine literature. Studies show also that using trade books to teach skills and strategies is very successful and that students do transfer this learning to their reading in other contexts.

About the Library Books Collection Teacher's Guide

The *Library Books Collection Teacher's Guide* provides inviting literacy activities for twelve diverse, high-quality trade books. Each trade book connects to a popular thematic unit and has a daily lesson plan that reinforces reading skills and strategies. These daily student-centered lessons make it easy to include trade books as part of a rich, well-balanced reading program.

Features of Lesson Plans

- reproducible pages for daily instruction

- focus skills and strategies that correlate with *Trophies*

- theme connections that correlate with themes in *Trophies*

- vocabulary study and Language Links

- Response Journal activities

- Book Talk questions for guided reading

- Wrap-Up Projects and Inquiry Projects

- writing activities that include narrative, informative, and persuasive writing

Additional Program Features

- bookmarks, role badges, and record-keeping instruments for Literature Circles

- The Traits of Good Writing and writing rubrics

- additional vocabulary activities

- learning contracts

Using the Library Books Collection

Using the Library Books Collection with *Trophies*

There are a number of options for using the trade books in the Library Books Collection and the accompanying lessons in the *Library Books Collection Teacher's Guide* to supplement, complement, or expand upon your students' reading in *Trophies*. Because the trade books are theme-related, you can use them in conjunction with the anthology without interrupting your theme-based instruction.

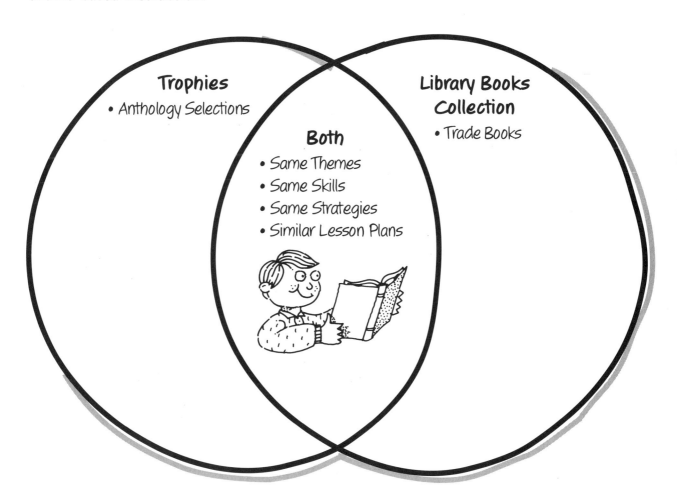

Trophies
- Anthology Selections

Both
- Same Themes
- Same Skills
- Same Strategies
- Similar Lesson Plans

Library Books Collection
- Trade Books

Library Books that correlate with each *Trophies* theme are listed within the lessons of the *Teacher's Edition*. The Skills and Strategies Chart on page 6 shows how the focus skills and strategies in the Library Book lesson plans reinforce the focus skills and strategies in *Trophies*.

Skills and Strategies Chart

Each Library Book is paired with a theme from the *Trophies* Pupil Edition. Every trade book reinforces the focus skills and focus strategies taught in *Trophies*.

Theme	Library Book	Focus Skill	Focus Strategy
Theme 1: Look Inside	The Black Stallion	Prefixes, Suffixes, and Roots	Create Mental Images
	Sees Behind Trees	Narrative Elements	Reread to Clarify
Theme 2: Team Work	Baseball in the Barrios	Summarize and Paraphrase	Make and Confirm Predictions
	The Tarantula in My Purse	Draw Conclusions	Summarize
Theme 3: A Changing Planet	Maria's Comet	Text Structure: Main Idea and Details	Self-Question
	Stone Wall Secrets	Graphic Aids	Use Decoding/Phonics
Theme 4: Express Yourself	The Young Artist	Word Relationships	Make and Confirm Predictions
	Dear Benjamin Banneker	Fact and Opinion	Read Ahead
Theme 5: School Rules	Frindle	Text Structure: Compare and Contrast	Use Context to Confirm Meaning
	Beetles, Lightly Toasted	Author's Purpose and Perspective	Adjust Reading Rate
Theme 6: American Adventure	The Cat Who Escaped from Steerage	Text Structure: Cause and Effect	Summarize
	And Then What Happened, Paul Revere?	Connotation/Denotation	Self-Question

© Harcourt

Management Options

The Library Books and lesson plans can be used in a variety of
ways to fit your teaching style and the needs of your students.
The Library Books and the accompanying lessons in the *Library
Books Collection Teacher's Guide* can be used with whole groups or
small groups.

Whole Group

Expand on a theme by having students read theme-related
Library Books in addition to *Pupil Edition* selections.

Small Groups

1. Use challenging books from the Library Books Collection
   to allow above-level readers to proceed at their own pace
   or to pursue individual interests. You may want to establish
   a learning contract with the student if he or she will be
   completing the book and lesson plan independently. For
   more information and a sample learning contract, see
   pages 152–153.

2. Have below-level readers read a book at their reading level
   and complete the lesson plan with other students reading
   the same book. Student-centered lesson plans provide
   teachers with the opportunity to give additional support to
   those who need it.

3. Have small mixed groups of students read a Library Book
   that interests them. Discussion groups and cooperative
   activities provide below-level readers with
   peer support while providing above-level
   readers with the opportunity to take part
   in thought-provoking discussions and
   hands-on activities.

4. Have students read in Literature Circles.
   See pages 9–10 for suggestions on using
   Literature Circles in the classroom.

Other Ways to Use the Library Books Collection

In Leveled Order

- Students may read individually, with partners, or in small groups.
- For information and suggestions on providing students with appropriate texts and assessing their progress, see the Library Book Levels section on page 15.

In Your Classroom Library

- Have Library Books available for independent self-selected reading. Duplicate daily lessons for students to complete independently.
- Encourage groups of students to form informal book clubs based on shared interest in a self-selected book. Students meet on a regular basis to read and discuss the book they've chosen.

Sustained Silent Reading (SSR)

- Set aside 15 to 30 minutes each day and have students read silently from a Library Book.
- Reinforce what is being read by discussing the Library Books as a class, or by having students use the My Reading Log form, found on page R38 of the *Teacher's Edition*.

For Cross-Curricular Connections

- Choose Library Books that you can link to units you are teaching in science, social studies, math, music, art, and other areas.
- Use Library Books to introduce, support, and extend your teaching of content-area units.

> *"As proficiency develops, reading should be thought of not so much as a separate subject in school but as integral to learning literature, social studies, and science."*
>
> **The Commission on Reading**
> *Becoming a Nation of Readers*

Literature Circles

Literature Circles are small groups of students who come together to read and respond to a piece of literature of their choice. The Literature Circle approach is an excellent way to integrate quality trade books and collaborative learning into a classroom reading program.

◎ **Getting Started** Select trade books that reflect students' interests. Give a brief presentation to introduce each of the books. Use students' book choices as the basis for forming Literature Circles.

◎ **Scheduling Literature Circles** Set up a schedule for Literature Circles to meet on a regular basis. You might divide each session into periods for reading, writing, and discussion; or you may prefer to rotate sessions devoted to reading and writing with group meetings on alternate days.

◎ **Conducting Literature Circles** Students determine a reasonable number of pages to read for each session. After they read each day's portion, they write responses to what they have just read. Then they use their written responses to launch a discussion of the day's reading. The **Literature Circle Bookmarks** on pages 145–146 provide questions that students might ask themselves to guide their reading and discussion. When the group has finished their book, they decide on an interesting and creative way to share it with classmates and perhaps to interest others in reading it. Have students use the **Literature Circle Checklist** on page 151 to monitor their own participation in Literature Circles and to remind them of their responsibilities as members of the group.

◎ **Using Roles** When Literature Circles are relatively new, it is helpful to have students take turns assuming a variety of task roles to guide and focus their reading, writing, and discussion. You may assign roles or allow students to choose their own.

Literature Circle Role Badges can be found on pages 147–150. The badges show eight possible roles for both fiction and non-fiction, with a brief description of each role on the reverse side of the badge. After students complete their daily reading, have them make notes about the literature from the perspective of their role for that day. They can then bring their notes to contribute to the discussion.

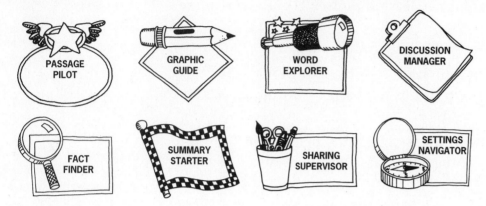

🌀 **Using Journals** After students have become familiar with Literature Circles, you can eliminate the roles and instead have students write entries in their response journals to use as a springboard for discussion.

🌀 **Promoting Free Discussion** Guide students to understand that their roles or journal notes are meant to provide a springboard for discussion rather than a formula that must be followed. Encourage group members to engage in conversations that allow for spontaneous observations and responses.

🌀 **Introducing Procedures and Concepts** The ultimate goal is for students to conduct Literature Circles on their own. However, they may first require guidance and practice. One way to familiarize students with the concepts and practices is by using brief selections for practice sessions during which you model good discussion questions, responses that enrich the discussion, and effective group dynamics. Help students learn to use the roles by focusing on one role at a time.

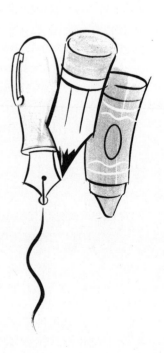

🌀 **Assessing Students' Progress** Literature Circles lend themselves to informal observation and assessment. The **Literature Circle Student Record Form** on page 144 provides a convenient means for assessing students' progress.

Journaling

How to Use Journals

Journaling has become a valuable tool widely used in today's classroom. The following chart shows how you might use some popular types of journals.

TYPE OF JOURNAL	HOW IT'S USED	POSSIBLE SCHEDULING
daily journal	Students record their experiences, feelings, and ideas.	at the beginning of the school day
learning log	Students write their reflections on content-area learning.	at the end of a class session or study unit
response journal (reading log, literature log)	Students write responses to what they are reading.	during/after each reading session

More About Response Journals

When writing in response journals, students should record the title of the book they are reading and their thoughts and feelings about what they have just read. It may be helpful to ask some guiding questions, such as:

- What did you like best and least about the part you just read, and why?

- What thoughts do you have about the characters and what they did?

- What questions did you ask yourself as you were reading?

- What did you picture in your mind as you were reading?

- What do you predict might happen next?

Journaling as a Springboard for Literature Circles

After students have become familiar with Literature Circles and comfortable with participating in them, role sheets can be replaced by personal response journals. During and after reading, students can record their responses and ideas for discussion topics in their journals to bring to the literature circle meeting.

Genre

Why is it important to learn about genre?

Students should know and understand that there are many genres and that each one offers different and exciting approaches to literature. Learning about genre helps students become more effective and successful readers. Knowing the characteristics of each genre improves students' comprehension by empowering them to set appropriate purposes for reading and to interpret information based on those purposes. When students understand that texts of different genres have different forms and functions, they are able to engage in reading and be active, knowledgeable readers.

What are the different types of genres?

Students should become familiar with the distinguishing characteristics of each major genre and the purposes, or goals, authors often associate with each one.

⊚ **autobiography:** The story of a real person's life, told by that person. The author's purpose is usually to express thoughts and feelings, not just give information.

⊚ **biography:** The story of a real person's life, told by someone else. The purpose is to inform, but the author may invent some details, such as dialogue, to bring the person to life.

⊚ **fantasy:** A fanciful story about events that could not really happen. The purpose is to entertain, but the story may also have a message.

⊚ **mystery:** A story in which the main character and the reader are challenged to solve a problem. The purpose is to entertain.

⊚ **nonfiction:** Information about a particular topic which often includes photos, captions, or diagrams. The author's purpose is to give factual information.

⊚ **realistic fiction:** A made-up story. The characters and events in the story often imitate real life.

⊚ **science fiction:** A story based on ideas from science. The plot is unrealistic, and the story is usually set in the future.

You may choose to use titles from the Library Books Collection to examine the nuances of the different genres with students. For example, students may be familiar with the character Ramona Quimby from Beverly Cleary's *Ramona Quimby, Age 8*. Knowing that the trade book is realistic fiction can help students understand Ramona's actions by comparing them to their own. Historical fiction such as *When Willard Met Babe Ruth* can be used to elicit from students that although Babe Ruth was a real person, the events in the story were invented by the author.

How can I use the Library Books to teach about genre?

The chart on page 14 shows the genre designations for the trade books in the Library Books Collection. You can integrate Library Books into your teaching of genre in a number of ways. The graphic below shows some suggestions.

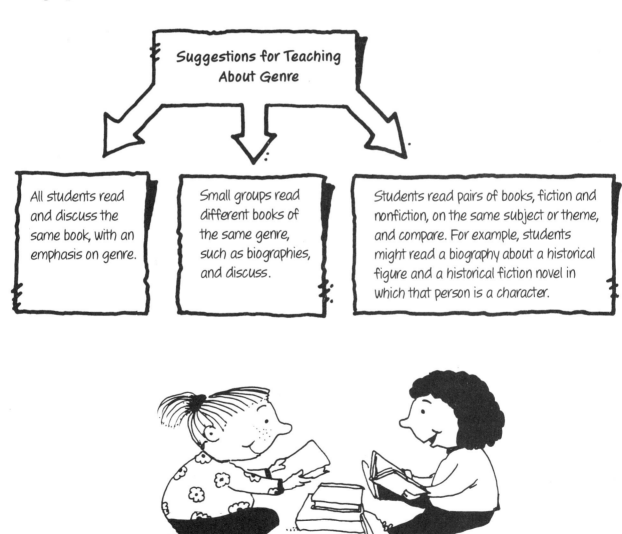

Suggestions for Teaching About Genre

All students read and discuss the same book, with an emphasis on genre.

Small groups read different books of the same genre, such as biographies, and discuss.

Students read pairs of books, fiction and nonfiction, on the same subject or theme, and compare. For example, students might read a biography about a historical figure and a historical fiction novel in which that person is a character.

Genre and Cross-Curricular Chart

Genre	Self-Discovery	Working Together	Growth and Change	Creativity	Communities	Explorations	Science	Social Studies	Language Arts	Math	The Arts
	Trophies Themes						Cross-Curricular Connections				
Realistic Fiction											
Frindle					•				•		
Sees Behind Trees	•							•			
The Black Stallion	•							•			
Beetles, Lightly Toasted				•			•				
Nonfiction											
The Tarantula in My Purse		•					•				
Biography											
And Then What Happened, Paul Revere?						•		•			
Baseball in the Barrios		•						•			
Dear Benjamin Banneker				•			•				
Historical Fiction											
Maria's Comet			•				•				
The Cat Who Escaped from Steerage						•		•			
Fantasy											
Stone Wall Secrets			•				•				
Folktales											
The Young Artist			•								•

Library Book Levels

The Library Books have been leveled using a consistent set of criteria, including the following:

PRIMARY LEVELS	PRIMARY AND INTERMEDIATE	INTERMEDIATE LEVELS
• illustrations • repetition of language patterns • language structures	• content • vocabulary • prior knowledge	• vocabulary concepts • genre • illustration or graphic support

Individual Reading Inventory Forms are provided for assessing students' reading progress at various times during the school year. For more information, see page 164.

- If the student reads the indicated passage from the selected Library Book with almost perfect accuracy, reassess him or her at a higher level and provide appropriate instruction with books from the Library Books Collection.
- If the student meets the criteria on page 164, he or she is ready to begin reading instruction at the indicated level.
- If the student makes too many errors, reassess him or her at a lower level and provide additional support.

Book Title	Library Book Level	Guided Reading Level	Lexile Level
Frindle	4.5–5.0	R	830
Maria's Comet	4.5–5.0	R	770
Sees Behind Trees	4.5–5.0	R	840
The Cat Who Escaped from Steerage	5.0–5.5	S–T	940
And Then What Happened, Paul Revere?	5.0–5.5	S–T	790
The Tarantula in My Purse	5.5–6.0	U–V	830
Baseball in the Barrios	5.5–6.0	U–V	940
The Black Stallion	5.5–6.0	U–V	680
Beetles, Lightly Toasted	6.0	V	950
Dear Benjamin Banneker	6.0–6.5	V–W	1100
Stone Wall Secrets	6.5–7.0	X–Y	620
The Young Artist	6.5–7.0	X–Y	790

The Black Stallion

by Walter Farley

Reading Level

▶ Theme Connection

As students read *The Black Stallion*, they will learn how a wild stallion saves a boy's life, leading to a powerful relationship between boy and horse. The boy discovers his own strengths when he teams up with the black stallion.

▶ Summary

When a ship goes down at sea, a wild black stallion pulls Alec Ramsay to safety on a desert island. There the two survivors develop a deep bond. Finally rescued and returned to New York, Alec and "the Black" meet Henry, a retired jockey and horse trainer, who is convinced that "the Black" can become a champion racehorse. Alec and his stallion overcome many obstacles and finally triumph.

▶ Building Background

Tell students that *The Black Stallion*, one of the most popular of all horse stories, is realistic fiction. Explain that the story explores the relationship between a boy and a stallion. Ask students to share any information they have about horses and any experiences they may have had with horses. Have students read to find out what happens to Alec and his horse.

Author Profile

Walter Farley published *The Black Stallion* in 1941, when he was an undergraduate at Columbia University. Critical acclaim and popularity with readers led him to write many sequels, as well as several other books about horses. In all, he wrote thirty-four books. Farley died in 1989, but his son, Steven Farley, has continued to write Black Stallion sequels.

Additional Books by the Author
- *The Black Stallion Returns*
- *The Black Stallion Mystery*
- *The Black Stallion's Courage*

Vocabulary

Have students use some of the vocabulary words to complete a simile sheet like the example shown below. Remind students that a simile is a comparison of two things using the words *like* or *as*. See pages 158–161 for additional vocabulary activities.

Simile Sheet

Word	Simile
lather	Lather formed on the horse's back like soap bubbling up in water.

Day 1	Day 2	Day 3	Day 4
lather p. 5	quivered p. 27	frantically p. 41	grooms p. 56
halter p. 6	canter p. 32	bedlam p. 47	restlessly p. 65
swerved p. 13	bolted p. 32		beseechingly p. 77

Day 5	Day 6	Day 7	Day 8
loping p. 86	contrary p. 116	momentum p. 134	commentator p. 180
spectators p. 104	skittishly p. 122	curbed p. 147	surging p. 183
dismounted p. 112	iodine p. 133	acclaiming p. 152	

© Harcourt

	Response	**Strategies**	**Skills**
Day 1 **Chapters** **1–2**	**Book Talk** • Characters' Emotions • Summarize • Important Details **Writing:** Personal Opinion	CREATE MENTAL IMAGES `FOCUS STRATEGY`	PREFIXES, SUFFIXES, AND ROOTS `FOCUS SKILL` *Distant Voyages* pp. T44–T45
Day 2 **Chapters** **3–4**	**Book Talk** • Characters' Traits • Important Details • Draw Conclusions **Writing:** Relate to Character	Reread to Clarify	Graphic Aids *Distant Voyages* pp. T294–T295
Day 3 **Chapters** **5–6**	**Book Talk** • Cause-Effect • Summarize • Compare and Contrast **Writing:** Respond to Story	Adjust Reading Rate	Classify/Categorize *Distant Voyages* pp. T421A–T421B
Day 4 **Chapters** **7–8**	**Book Talk** • Summarize • Important Details • Express Personal Opinions **Writing:** Personal Response	CREATE MENTAL IMAGES `FOCUS STRATEGY`	PREFIXES, SUFFIXES, AND ROOTS `FOCUS SKILL` *Distant Voyages* pp. T44–T45
Day 5 **Chapters** **9–11**	**Book Talk** • Characters' Emotions • Cause-Effect • Express Personal Opinions **Writing:** Personal Opinion	Use Text Structure and Format	Figurative Language *Distant Voyages* pp. T183A–T183B
Day 6 **Chapters** **12–13**	**Book Talk** • Draw Conclusions • Speculate • Make Predictions **Writing:** Personal Opinion	Use Context to Confirm Meaning	Fact and Opinion *Distant Voyages* pp. T420–T421
Day 7 **Chapters** **14–16**	**Book Talk** • Important Details • Summarize • Cause-Effect **Writing:** Relate to Character	Self-Question	Author's Purpose and Perspective *Distant Voyages* pp. T532–T533
Day 8 **Chapters** **17–18**	**Book Talk** • Make Comparisons • Theme • Identify with Characters **Writing:** Story	Use Text Structure and Format	Figurative Language *Distant Voyages* pp. T183A–T183B

Days **9–10** **Wrap-Up**	**Project** ✓ Design a Racing Board Game • Inquiry Project	**Writing** ✓ Story	**Language Link** • Communicating Without Words **Assessment** ✓ Comprehension Test

*Additional support is provided in *Trophies*.

✓ Options for Assessment

The Black Stallion

BOOK TALK

After you read Chapters 1 and 2, meet with your group to discuss and answer the following questions:

1 How do you think Alec feels the first time he sees the wild stallion?

2 How does the stallion save Alec's life after the shipwreck?

3 How does Alec's birthday gift from his uncle help him?

RESPONSE JOURNAL

Which part of Chapters 1 and 2 did you enjoy most? Why?

Strategies Good Readers Use

FOCUS STRATEGY **CREATE MENTAL IMAGES**

Picture in your mind Alec trying to survive after the shipwreck. How does this strategy help you when you read?

SKILLS IN CONTEXT

FOCUS SKILL **PREFIXES, SUFFIXES, AND ROOTS: BIG, BIGGER, BIGGEST WORDS GAME** Good readers decode long words by looking for parts of the word that they know, including spelling patterns, root words, prefixes, and suffixes.

What You Need

• pencil and paper
• index cards
• dictionary

What to Do

1. Revisit Chapters 1–2 of *The Black Stallion.* Write at least four root words, four prefixes, and four suffixes on index cards.

2. Make new words by combining each root word with prefixes and/or suffixes.

3. Record all the words that you make.

4. Use a dictionary to check spelling and to see if each word you form is a real word.

Here are some words with prefixes and suffixes to get you started: untamable, dreamed, wonderful

Think Ahead
What will happen to Alec on the island?

The Black Stallion

BOOK TALK

After you read Chapters 3 and 4, meet with your group to discuss and answer the following questions:

1 What tells you that Alec has good survival skills?

2 How does Alec begin to tame the stallion?

3 What might have attracted the ship to the island when it was out at sea?

RESPONSE JOURNAL

If you were Alec, how would you feel about your experiences on the island?

> **Strategies Good Readers Use**
>
> **REREAD TO CLARIFY**
>
> Good readers often reread passages with many details in them. What passages from Chapters 3 and 4 did you reread?

SKILLS IN CONTEXT

GRAPHIC AIDS: AN IMAGINARY ISLAND Graphic aids, such as photographs, charts, maps, and graphs, can make information easier to understand. Shortly before the storm in *The Black Stallion*, the ship is off the coast of Spain. Imagine that visitors want to go to the island where Alec and the stallion managed to survive. Create an imaginary island, and make a map to guide visitors around it.

What You Need

- reference sources or the Internet
- paper
- writing and drawing tools

What to Do

1. Look in reference sources that have maps of the coast of Spain and information about the area. Make notes about any features that could help you plan an imaginary island close to Spain.

2. Browse through Chapters 3 and 4 in *The Black Stallion*, and make notes about features on the island.

3. Create an imaginary island based on your research and on details in the story. Draw the island and use labels to identify places and things.

4. Give your imaginary island a name and compare your island with a classmate's island.

Here are some details from the story to get you started: Alec found a scrub tree; there was a cove.

Think Ahead
What will happen to the stallion now that help has arrived?

The Black Stallion

BOOK TALK

After you read Chapters 5 and 6, meet with your group to discuss and answer the following questions:

1 Why don't the sailors believe Alec's story at first?

2 How does the stallion get onto the boat?

3 What is the stallion like when Alec is around? How is he different when Alec is not nearby?

RESPONSE JOURNAL

How would you describe the relationship between Alec and the stallion at this point in the story?

> ### Strategies Good Readers Use
>
> **ADJUST READING RATE**
>
> Did you adjust your reading rate for any passages in *The Black Stallion?* Write a sentence explaining how slowing down when needed can help you understand what you are reading.

SKILLS IN CONTEXT

CLASSIFY/CATEGORIZE: WHERE DO THEY GO? Similar ideas can be grouped together. *The Black Stallion* includes many words that vividly describe the characters and the action. Find some of these words in Chapters 5 and 6. Then sort them into categories.

What You Need

- index cards or paper cut into squares
- paper
- writing materials

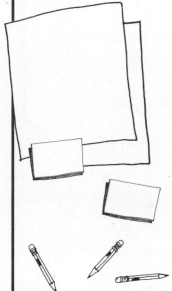

What to Do

1. Form groups. Browse through Chapters 5 and 6 and look for words that you feel paint a picture of what is happening. Find at least ten words, and write each on a card.

2. Work with your group to sort the cards into categories. You might begin with categories such as *Words That Describe Alec*, *Words That Describe the Stallion*, and *Words That Describe the Action*. Write the categories on separate pieces of paper, and sort the words according to where you think they belong.

3. After you have sorted the words once, mix them up and start over. Think of new categories or sort the words in a new way. For example, a word that describes Alec could also describe the stallion.

   Here are some words to get you started: *terrifying, bedlam, muzzle, frantically, strength*

Think Ahead
Will Alec and the stallion reach New York?

© Harcourt

The Black Stallion

BOOK TALK

After you read Chapters 7 and 8, meet with your group to discuss and answer the following questions:

1 Why does Alec have trouble unloading the stallion in New York? How does he solve the problem?

2 Who are these new characters: Henry, Tony, Napoleon, and Joe Russo?

3 Which of the new characters will be most important to the story? Why?

RESPONSE JOURNAL

How do you think your parents would feel if you arrived home with a horse?

Strategies Good Readers Use

FOCUS STRATEGY **CREATE MENTAL IMAGES**

Forming a picture in your mind as you read and thinking about what you already know can help you understand a story. Write a sentence telling where you have used this strategy in *The Black Stallion*.

SKILLS IN CONTEXT

FOCUS SKILL **PREFIXES, SUFFIXES, AND ROOTS: WHAT DOES IT MEAN?** When you come across a long word you do not know, try breaking the word into parts. Looking for word parts—prefixes, suffixes, and roots—can often help you figure out the unfamiliar word.

What You Need

- index cards
- writing tools
- colored pencils or markers
- dictionary

What to Do

1. Revisit *The Black Stallion* to find long words that are unfamiliar to you.

2. Write each word on a separate index card.

3. Draw colored lines to break the word into parts. Write the meanings of the parts you find.

4. Figure out a meaning for the word. Use a dictionary to check the definition.

5. Write the meaning on the back of the card, and illustrate the word, if possible.

6. Share your cards with a group of classmates. Try guessing the meanings of each other's words.

Here are some words to get you started: murmured, circulating, tenderly

Think Ahead How will the stallion react to his new life?

© Harcourt

The Black Stallion

BOOK TALK

After you read Chapters 9–11, meet with your group to discuss and answer the following questions:

1 Why is Henry so interested in helping Alec train and ride the stallion?

2 Why might Henry be nervous about the possibility of getting the stallion into a race?

3 Do you think that the stallion would allow anyone but Alec to ride him? Why or why not?

RESPONSE JOURNAL

Is training a horse an experience you have had or would like to have? Explain.

Strategies Good Readers Use

USE TEXT STRUCTURE AND FORMAT

Write two sentences explaining how a novel and a reference book are different in text structure and format.

SKILLS IN CONTEXT

FIGURATIVE LANGUAGE: WINNER'S WREATH   Figurative language conveys meaning beyond the literal meaning of a word or phrase. Writers often use figurative language to enhance descriptions. Hyperbole, simile, metaphor, and imagery are types of figurative language. Explore figurative language in *The Black Stallion* by creating a wreath of figurative language.

What You Need

- **notebook paper**
- **pencil**
- **colored construction paper**
- **scissors**
- **black pen**
- **hole punch**
- **chenille sticks or yarn**

What to Do

1. Revisit Chapters 9–11. Note examples of figurative language. Write each example as a brief sentence. (Be sure to include the figurative language.) Circle ten examples to use in your wreath.

2. Outline ten flower shapes on different colors of construction paper. Cut them out.

3. With a black pen, copy one example of figurative language onto each flower.

4. Punch holes at the top and bottom of each flower. Connect the flowers with chenille sticks or pieces of yarn. Your wreath should be shaped like a horseshoe.

5. Display your wreath in the classroom.

Here is an example of figurative language to get you started: The stallion's mane whipped behind him like waves of smoke.

Think Ahead
How will Henry and Alec try to train the stallion?

© Harcourt

The Black Stallion

BOOK TALK

After you read Chapters 12 and 13, meet with your group to discuss and answer the following questions:

1 Why might Napoleon have a calming effect on the stallion?

2 Why do Henry and Alec go to Belmont during the night rather than during the day?

3 Will Henry find out that the stallion is registered? Explain your answer.

RESPONSE JOURNAL

Would you take the chances Alec is taking? Why or why not?

> ### Strategies Good Readers Use
>
> **USE CONTEXT TO CONFIRM MEANING**
>
> Find the word *skittishly* on page 122. Use context clues to figure out the word's meaning. Write what you think *skittishly* means.

SKILLS IN CONTEXT

FACT AND OPINION: FACT AND OPINION GAME Facts are ideas that can be proven. Opinions are ideas that are personal beliefs. Opinions can differ from person to person. Revisit Chapters 12 and 13 of *The Black Stallion* to find ideas that are facts and other ideas that are opinions. Then make a fact and opinion game.

What You Need

- index cards or paper cut into squares
- writing tools

What to Do

1. Look through Chapters 12 and 13. Find ten ideas that are either facts or opinions. Write each as a statement on a separate card. Write *F* or *O* in the bottom corner of the card.

2. Play the game with a classmate. One player is the caller, and the other is the contestant. The caller reads his or her statements, one at a time. The contestant tells if the statement is a fact or an opinion. If the answer is correct, the contestant gets the card. If not, the caller keeps the card.

3. Give reasons for labeling the card *F* or *O* if you disagree about which statements are facts or opinions. Discuss any statements you feel could be both a fact and an opinion.

4. Switch roles and play the game again.

Here are some examples to get you started: *The stallion reared. (fact) He's as wild as they come. (opinion)*

Think Ahead Will Alec get to ride the stallion in a race?

© Harcourt

The Black Stallion

BOOK TALK

After you read Chapters 14–16, meet with your group to discuss and answer the following questions:

1. What problems do Alec and Henry have with getting the stallion into a race?

2. How does sports columnist Jim Neville help out?

3. At the end of Chapter 15, Alec feels cool and composed rather than excited. Why do you think he feels this way?

Strategies Good Readers Use

SELF-QUESTION

Good readers ask themselves questions as they read. Write two questions that you asked yourself as you read Chapters 14–16 of *The Black Stallion*.

RESPONSE JOURNAL

If you were Alec, how would you feel about the race?

SKILLS IN CONTEXT

AUTHOR'S PURPOSE AND PERSPECTIVE: PERSPECTIVE PUZZLE To determine the author's perspective, ask yourself: *What is the author's opinion or attitude about the subject? What is the author's purpose for expressing this opinion or attitude?* Horse racing is an important part of the plot in *The Black Stallion*. Use clues from the book to determine the author's perspective about horse racing.

What You Need

- **notebook paper**
- **construction paper**
- **writing materials**
- **scissors**

What to Do

1. Look again at Chapters 14–16. Jot down words or phrases that the author uses to describe horse racing. Use these words and phrases to help you determine how the author feels about horse racing.

2. Draw puzzle-shaped pieces on a sheet of construction paper. On each piece, write one of the words or phrases that describes horse racing.

3. On the back of the paper, write a sentence that tells the author's perspective about horse racing.

4. Cut your puzzle into pieces and exchange puzzles with a classmate.

5. Put each other's puzzles together and compare your statements of perspective. Did you agree about how the author feels about racing?

Here's an idea to get you started: *"...the greatest excitement in the sports world today is being caused by two of the fastest horses ever to set foot on any track, Cyclone and Sun Raider."*

Think Ahead
What will happen at the race?

© Harcourt

The Black Stallion

BOOK TALK

After you read Chapters 17 and 18, meet with your group to discuss and answer the following questions:

1 How is Alec like characters from selections you have read in *Distant Voyages*?

2 What are some themes in *The Black Stallion*?

3 How do you think Alec felt during and after the race?

RESPONSE JOURNAL

Would you want to ride a horse like the black stallion in a race? Explain.

Strategies Good Readers Use

USE TEXT STRUCTURE AND FORMAT

Examine the first four paragraphs on page 175 of *The Black Stallion*. How do the dashes and dots help you understand the dialogue? Write your answer.

SKILLS IN CONTEXT

FIGURATIVE LANGUAGE: AN OVERSTATED STALLION Figurative language is used to create effects, emphasize ideas, and convey emotions. Hyperbole is an exaggeration or overstatement used for special effect. Revisit Chapters 17 and 18 in *The Black Stallion*. Notice how excited the sports commentator sounds. He might have used hyperbole such as "That horse could run to the moon!" Use story events to create hyperbole of your own.

What You Need

- **large paper**
- **writing paper**
- **construction paper cut into strips**
- **writing and drawing tools**
- **glue or tape**

What to Do

1. On writing paper, jot down a few examples of hyperbole based on the story. Choose the one you like best.

2. Select a strip of construction paper. Write your example of hyperbole on it and add decorations.

3. Work with your classmates to make a hyperbole display. Glue or tape the strips of construction paper to the large paper.

Here is an example of hyperbole to get you started:
The stallion could run for a million years.

The Stallion could run for a million years.

Wrap-Up

▶ **Project** **DESIGN A RACING BOARD GAME** Recall with students the exciting race that takes place at the end of *The Black Stallion*. Tell students that they can use a horse race as the basis for a board game that they create.

- Organize students into groups and have them discuss the components of a board game.
- Ask students to complete the copying master on page 27 to plan their games.
- Have each group design an original horse racing game using what they learned from reading *The Black Stallion*, along with any other information they need.
- Have each group present its finished game to the class.

▶ **Writing** **STORY** Have students respond to the following writing prompt: **Write a story describing a new adventure for Alec and the stallion.** Have students use the copying master on page 28 to plan their story. Remind students to focus on interesting ideas for their story. Rubrics for evaluating student writing are provided on pages 154–157.

▶ **Language Link** **COMMUNICATING WITHOUT WORDS** Point out to students that Alec uses different ways of communicating with the stallion. Ask students to write a brief description of nonverbal ways they might communicate a message to a friend.

Inquiry Project

The Black Stallion can be a springboard for inquiry into a variety of topics and ideas. Have students brainstorm topics they would like to know more about and organize their responses in a list. Students can use reference books and the Internet to begin their inquiry projects.

> **The Black Stallion**
>
> - horses
> - training horses
> - race horses
> - horses in the wild
> - animal-human relationships

✔ **Comprehension Test** Test students' comprehension of *The Black Stallion* by having them complete the copying master on page 29.

Name _____

Project Planner

The Black Stallion ends with an exciting horse race that the stallion wins. Design a horse racing board game based on what you learned from reading the story.

☐ **Step 1.** Talk with your group about what you need to know to design your game. Discuss what you learned about horse racing from reading *The Black Stallion*. If you need more information, choose the reference sources you will use. Discuss these questions:

- How many horses might run in a race?
- What are some of the rules for a race?

What You Need

- poster board
- index cards or paper cut into squares
- construction paper
- writing and drawing materials
- reference sources

☐ **Step 2.** Brainstorm ideas for the game. Use the chart below to record your ideas.

Horse Racing Game		
Rules	Board Design	Movement Cards

☐ **Step 3.** Work together to create your game. Use poster board to make a game board. Make cards that direct movement around the board. Create small horses from different colors of construction paper for players to move around the board. Write a list of rules for your game.

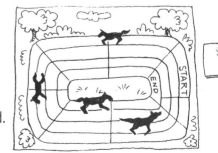

☐ **Step 4.** Play your game. Make any changes you think are needed.

☐ **Step 5.** Present your game to the class.

© Harcourt

Story

Write a story about a new adventure for Alec and the stallion. Use what you know about both characters as you plan your story. Complete the graphic organizer to help you plan your story.

Prewriting Graphic Organizer

Characters _____

_____

Setting _____

_____

Problem _____

_____

Important Events _____

_____

_____

_____

_____

_____

Solution _____

_____

© Harcourt

Name _____

Comprehension Test

Read each question below. Then mark the letter for the answer you have chosen.

1. **What interrupts Alec's trip home?**
   - Ⓐ a visit to Spain
   - Ⓑ a hurricane at sea
   - Ⓒ a shipwreck
   - Ⓓ mechanical problems on the ship

2. **How does Alec get to an island?**
   - Ⓕ The stallion tows him there.
   - Ⓖ The ship drops him off.
   - Ⓗ He swims.
   - Ⓙ He floats on a raft.

3. **What does Alec accomplish on the island?**
   - Ⓐ He learns how to fish.
   - Ⓑ He builds a tree house.
   - Ⓒ He begins to tame the stallion.
   - Ⓓ He builds a tower from stones.

4. **What does Henry want to do with the stallion?**
   - Ⓕ enter him in horse shows
   - Ⓖ train him and enter him in races
   - Ⓗ turn him over to a circus
   - Ⓙ take him to New Jersey

5. **What concerns Henry about the stallion?**
   - Ⓐ its size
   - Ⓑ its color
   - Ⓒ its previous owner
   - Ⓓ its registration papers

6. **Why do Henry and Alec go to Belmont?**
   - Ⓕ to see a race
   - Ⓖ to let the stallion run on a race track
   - Ⓗ to show the stallion to other people
   - Ⓙ to take pictures

7. **What does Jim Neville do?**
   - Ⓐ He finds a new owner for the stallion.
   - Ⓑ He gets the stallion a part in a movie.
   - Ⓒ He arranges for the stallion to run in a race.
   - Ⓓ He offers to buy the stallion.

8. **What does Alec do in Chicago?**
   - Ⓕ He visits his aunt.
   - Ⓖ He rides the stallion in a race.
   - Ⓗ He takes a tour of the city.
   - Ⓙ He goes to the hospital.

9. **What happens at the end of the story?**
   - Ⓐ Alec goes back to the island.
   - Ⓑ The stallion runs away.
   - Ⓒ Alec rides the stallion in a race and wins.
   - Ⓓ Alec goes to the Kentucky Derby.

10. **On a separate sheet of paper, write a short answer in response to the question below.**

    Do you think anyone besides Alec will ever be able to ride the stallion? Explain.

Sees Behind Trees

Reading Level

by Michael Dorris

Author Profile

Born in Louisville, Kentucky, in 1945, Michael Dorris was a leading literary voice of Native American culture who spent most of his life teaching and writing. Dorris often collaborated with his wife, writer Louise Erdrich.

Additional Books by the Author
- *Morning Girl*
- *Guests*
- *The Window*

Theme Connection As students read the full-length version of *Sees Behind Trees*, they will learn how Walnut uses his remarkable powers of observation both to help others and to move closer to adulthood.

Summary Because Walnut's eyesight is poor, his mother helps him to see in other ways. At his coming-of-age ceremony, Walnut proves that he can see "what cannot be seen" and earns the adult name Sees Behind Trees. He uses his skill when Gray Fire asks for help in finding his own vision, his own destiny.

Building Background Tell students that *Sees Behind Trees* is a historical fiction novel that takes place in North America in the sixteenth century—before the time of European settlement. The characters are imaginary, but the way they live is based on information about Native American life at that time. Explain that the novel they are about to read tells of a Native American boy who cannot see well and depends on his other senses. Have them read to find out what kinds of things the boy "sees" without his eyes.

Vocabulary

Help students record the vocabulary words in a Vocabulary Log like the one shown below. Encourage them to add other story words that puzzle or interest them. See pages 158–161 for additional vocabulary activities.

Vocabulary Log

Word	Meaning	Use it in a sentence
anxious	worried	I get anxious before tests.
pemmican	mixture of dried fat, berries, meat	Native Americans ate pemmican when they traveled.

Day 1	Day 2	Day 3	Day 4
anxious p. 1	mistrustful p. 23	criticism p. 52	mimicked p. 75
pemmican p. 1	insistent p. 24	disrespectful p. 56	peevishly p. 77
surrender p. 3	disguised p. 34	denied p. 59	gorge p. 80
awl p. 14	poultice p. 43	distinct p. 61	distinguishable p. 86

	Response	Strategies	Skills
Day 1 Chapters 1–2	**Book Talk** • Draw Conclusions • Important Details • Interpret Story Events **Writing:** Personal Response	**REREAD TO CLARIFY** `FOCUS STRATEGY`	**NARRATIVE ELEMENTS** `FOCUS SKILL` *Distant Voyages,* pp. T68–T69
Day 2 Chapters 3–4	**Book Talk** • Make Comparisons • Important Details • Speculate **Writing:** Personal Response	Summarize	Prefixes, Suffixes, and Roots *Distant Voyages,* pp. T44–T45
Day 3 Chapters 5–6	**Book Talk** • Important Details • Main Idea • Cause-Effect **Writing:** Personal Response	Make and Confirm Predictions	Summarize and Paraphrase *Distant Voyages,* pp. T182–T183
Day 4 Chapters 7–9	**Book Talk** • Make Comparisons • Interpret Theme • Speculate **Writing:** Personal Response	**REREAD TO CLARIFY** `FOCUS STRATEGY`	**NARRATIVE ELEMENTS** `FOCUS SKILL` *Distant Voyages,* pp. T68–T69

Day 5
Wrap-Up

Project
✓ Write and Perform a One-Act Play
• Inquiry Project

Writing
✓ Descriptive Paragraph

Language Link
Poetic Language

Assessment
✓ Comprehension Test

*Additional support is provided in *Trophies.*
✓ Options for Assessment

Sees Behind Trees

BOOK TALK

After you read Chapters 1 and 2, meet with your group to discuss and answer the following questions:

1 Why is Walnut worried when his mother stops teaching him to shoot moss out of the air?

2 How does Walnut's mother teach him to "see behind trees"?

3 Why do you think the test for someone who can see behind trees is held first?

RESPONSE JOURNAL

Imagine that you must pass some kind of test to receive an adult name. What kind of test would it be? What name do you think you would receive?

Strategies Good Readers Use

FOCUS STRATEGY **REREAD TO CLARIFY**

*I*f you have difficulty understanding how Walnut's mother teaches him to "see behind trees," reread Chapters 1 and 2. Rereading to clarify this information will help you to better enjoy the rest of the book.

SKILLS IN CONTEXT

FOCUS SKILL **NARRATIVE ELEMENTS: NAME POEM** Authors show the personality of characters in many ways. Often they do this through the actions, words, and thoughts of the character. Other times the personality of a character is revealed by the way other characters react to him or her. Use what you have learned about your favorite character's personality to write a name poem about that character.

What You Need

- lined paper
- crayons or markers
- pencil
- construction paper
- glue or tape

What to Do

1. Choose a character to write about. Look through Chapters 1 and 2 of *Sees Behind Trees* to review what the story tells you about that character.

2. Write the letters of your character's name one at a time from top to bottom on the page.

3. Write a descriptive word or phrase about the character on each line. Begin with the letter that appears on that line.

4. Illustrate your poem and mount it on a sheet of construction paper.

Here is a phrase to get you started:

Wishes he could see clearly (for the first letter of Walnut's name)

Think Ahead
How do you think life will change for Walnut now that he has an adult name?

Sees Behind Trees

BOOK TALK

After you read Chapters 3 and 4, meet with your group to discuss and answer the following questions:

1 How is Sees Behind Trees's life the same and different after he receives his grown-up name?

2 How does Sees Behind Trees feel about Gray Fire's story?

3 What does Gray Fire mean when he says, "I want to go back and look for what I left in the land of water"?

RESPONSE JOURNAL

Sees Behind Trees doesn't completely understand the dividing line between being a boy and being a man. Explain your thoughts about what will have to happen to make you feel like you have become a grown-up.

Strategies Good Readers Use

SUMMARIZE

In your own words, write a short paragraph that tells what has happened in these chapters. How does using this strategy help you understand and remember what you have read?

SKILLS IN CONTEXT

PREFIXES, SUFFIXES, AND ROOTS: PREFIX AND SUFFIX CONSTRUCTION GAME A prefix is a word part added to the beginning of a word. A suffix is a word part added to the end of a word. Adding a prefix or suffix to a root word creates a new word with a different meaning.

What You Need

- paper
- pencil
- 20–30 small index cards
- red, blue, and green markers
- timer
- dictionary

What to Do

1. Find words from Chapters 3–4 that include prefixes, suffixes, or both. Write each root word, suffix, and prefix.

2. On separate index cards, write 4–5 different prefixes; 5–7 different suffixes; and 10–15 different root words.

3. Get ready to play with a friend. Put all the cards in one pile and shuffle.

4. Deal half of the cards, facedown, to each player. Set the timer for two minutes. Turn your cards over. Combine root words with prefixes and suffixes. Each time you make a word, write it on your paper. The player with the most words wins. You can use the cards more than once.

Here are some words to get you started:
amazingly, comfortable, perfectly, unmistakable

Think Ahead
Will Sees Behind Trees find the land of water?

Sees Behind Trees

BOOK TALK

After you read Chapters 5 and 6, meet with your group to discuss and answer the following questions:

1 How does Sees Behind Trees's father show his concern for his son's safety on the journey?

2 How does Gray Fire teach Sees Behind Trees to find his way in the forest?

3 What does Sees Behind Trees's reaction to meeting strangers tell you about him and his people?

Strategies Good Readers Use

MAKE AND CONFIRM PREDICTIONS

Good readers make predictions about what will happen in the story. They confirm their predictions as they read. Write three predictions you made as you read Chapters 5–6.

RESPONSE JOURNAL

Because Sees Behind Trees has never seen a person he didn't already know, the idea of meeting strangers frightens him. Write a journal entry about a time when you had to go somewhere where there were many strangers. How did you feel? What were your thoughts?

SKILLS IN CONTEXT

SUMMARIZE AND PARAPHRASE: STORY TIME LINE Revisit Chapters 1–6 of the book to summarize the events that have taken place so far and create an illustrated time line.

What You Need

- index cards
- pencil or pen
- crayons or markers
- string, cut into 6" lengths
- scissors
- hole punch

What to Do

1. Write a sentence about each key story event on a separate index card.

2. Add an illustration to each card.

3. Punch a hole at the top and bottom of each card.

4. Connect the cards in order by tying a string through the holes in the top and bottom of each card.

5. Hang up your time line.

Here is a sentence to get you started:

Walnut's mother taught him to see what other people could not see.

Think Ahead

How do you think Sees Behind Trees will feel about the land of water when he sees it for the first time?

© Harcourt

Sees Behind Trees

BOOK TALK

Have students meet with their groups to discuss and answer the following questions:

1 How is Sees Behind Trees similar to another character you have read about in *Distant Voyages?*

2 What do you think is the most important theme in the story?

3 How do you think Sees Behind Trees's trip to the land of water will affect his life in the future?

RESPONSE JOURNAL

After Gray Fire goes over the cliff, Sees Behind Trees is pulled between what he should do and what he wants to do. Write a journal entry about a time when you had to choose between acting the way you knew you should or doing as you pleased.

Strategies Good Readers Use

FOCUS STRATEGY REREAD TO CLARIFY

Review pages 75–104 and look for passages from the story that you had trouble understanding. Reread those passages to clarify any information you might have overlooked the first time you read them.

SKILLS IN CONTEXT

FOCUS SKILL **NARRATIVE ELEMENTS: CHARACTER MOBILE** Because Sees Behind Trees tells the story, the author doesn't describe him directly. You learn about him through his own thoughts, words, and actions—and through the words and actions of others.

What You Need

- **construction paper in two different colors**
- **index cards**
- **crayons or markers**
- **wire coat hanger**
- **string**
- **scissors**
- **glue**

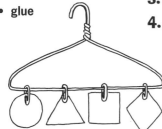

What to Do

1. Look through the book for things Sees Behind Trees says, thinks, and does that give hints about the kind of person he is. Write these examples—in your own words—on squares cut from paper of one color.

2. Then find examples of words and actions of other characters that also tell about Sees Behind Trees. Write these on circles cut from the second color of paper.

3. Add illustrations to the blank sides of the shapes.

4. Punch a hole at the center top of each shape and use string to attach the shapes to the hanger.

Here are some ideas to get you started:
Sees Behind Trees feels that he is not the person everyone thinks he is. Sees Behind Trees is not sure of his own abilities.

© Harcourt

Wrap-Up

▶ **Project** WRITE AND PERFORM A ONE-ACT PLAY *Sees Behind Trees* includes scenes that students would enjoy bringing to life in the form of one-act plays to present to other classes. Before groups begin their play projects, discuss the components of a play: actors, dialogue, stage directions, and props. (Explain that costumes are not required for this project.) Also model the format in which a play is written.

- Organize students into groups and have them choose a section of the book to rewrite in play form.
- Ask each group to complete the copying master on page 37 to plan their play.
- Have each group write their play in script form and create simple props.
- Provide time for practicing and performing the plays.

▶ **Writing** DESCRIPTIVE PARAGRAPH Have students respond to the following writing prompt: **Based on what you have read, describe the "land of water."** Tell students to focus on word choice. Have students use the copying master on page 38 to plan their paragraph. In addition, rubrics for evaluating student writing are provided on pages 154–157.

▶ **Language Link** POETIC LANGUAGE Point out to students that the author uses phrases and images that often seem like poetry. Have students reread Gray Fire's description of the land of water on pages 38–39. Then have students choose one image to rewrite in the form of a short rhymed or unrhymed poem.

Inquiry Project

Sees Behind Trees can be a springboard for inquiry into one or more of the different Native American tribes that inhabited Northeastern America prior to the arrival of European settlers. Before beginning the inquiry, have students complete the first two columns of a K-W-L chart like the one below. Explain that they can record information from *Sees Behind Trees* and other facts they already know in the first column. Their inquiry questions should be recorded in the second column. Have students use reference books and the Internet to find answers to their questions. This information can be added to the last column.

K What I Know	W What I Want to Find Out	L What I Learned
Sees Behind Trees is part of the Powhatan tribe.	What other Native American tribes lived in Northeastern America?	

✔ **Comprehension Test** Test students' comprehension of *Sees Behind Trees* by having them complete the copying master on page 39.

Name _____

Project Planner

Many of the scenes described in *Sees Behind Trees* are perfect for presenting in play form. Work in your group to write, practice, and perform a one-act play based on the book.

☐ **Step 1.** As a group, choose a section of *Sees Behind Trees* that you would like to rewrite in play form. Keep in mind that your finished play should take no more than five to ten minutes to perform. Record information about your section below.

What You Need
- paper
- pencils
- materials to create props
- poster paper

Characters: _____

Props Needed: _____

☐ **Step 2.** Work together to rewrite the selection in play form.
Then find or create simple props. For example, a quiver can be made from rolled construction paper. Also create a poster to advertise your play.

☐ **Step 3.** Assign group members to the roles listed below. (Roles with an asterisk beside them can be combined.) Practice the play at least once. You can make copies of the play and read the parts, so the lines do not have to be memorized.

Actors/Characters played: _____

_____

*Director: _____

*Prop Master: _____

*Announcer: _____

☐ **Step 4.** As a group, perform your play for an audience.

Descriptive Paragraph

Based on what you have read, describe the "land of water." Use the graphic organizer below to help you plan your paragraph. In the space for each sense, write words and phrases the author uses that appeal to that sense. When you finish, circle the images that seem most powerful to you. Then write your paragraph, using your own ideas and some of these images.

Prewriting Graphic Organizer

Sight: _____

_____

_____

Hearing: _____

_____

_____

Touch: _____

_____

_____

Smell: _____

_____

_____

© Harcourt

Name _____

Comprehension Test

Read each question below. Then mark the letter for the answer you have chosen.

1. **Why can't Walnut shoot moss out of the air?**
   - Ⓐ His bowstring is too tight.
   - Ⓑ His mother doesn't throw the moss well.
   - Ⓒ He can't see well.
   - Ⓓ He does not practice enough.

2. **Why is Frog called Three Chances?**
   - Ⓕ He is the third son in his family.
   - Ⓖ It takes him three tries to shoot the moss.
   - Ⓗ He shoots three pieces of moss.
   - Ⓙ He is one of Walnut's three best friends.

3. **Why is Sees Behind Trees the first person Gray Fire tells about the land of water?**
   - Ⓐ He thinks that Sees Behind Trees can find the land of water.
   - Ⓑ Sees Behind Trees is his only grandson.
   - Ⓒ He wants to pass the story on.
   - Ⓓ He thinks that Sees Behind Trees has seen the land of water.

4. **Why doesn't Sees Behind Trees tell his uncle where he is going?**
   - Ⓕ He is angry at his uncle.
   - Ⓖ Gray Fire does not want anyone else to know about the land of water.
   - Ⓗ His uncle does not treat him like a grown-up.
   - Ⓙ He is afraid his uncle won't let him go.

5. **Why is Sees Behind Trees frightened when he first sees Karna and Pitew?**
   - Ⓐ He cannot understand them.
   - Ⓑ He thinks that they are ghosts.
   - Ⓒ They are living too close to his village.
   - Ⓓ He has never seen a stranger before.

6. **How does Sees Behind Trees always start his day?**
   - Ⓕ He listens to the world around him.
   - Ⓖ He gets up as soon as he wakes.
   - Ⓗ He opens his eyes and tries to see the sun.
   - Ⓙ He bathes in the cold stream.

7. **What happens when Sees Behind Trees looks out at the land of water?**
   - Ⓐ His eyes start to sting.
   - Ⓑ His legs start to shake.
   - Ⓒ He can see things clearly.
   - Ⓓ He feels dizzy.

8. **Why doesn't Sees Behind Trees want to stay forever in the land of water?**
   - Ⓕ He knows Gray Fire wants to be alone.
   - Ⓖ He can't see anything in the mist.
   - Ⓗ He would miss his family and the village.
   - Ⓙ Gray Fire tells him he should go home.

9. **What does Sees Behind Trees think happened to Karna and Pitew?**
   - Ⓐ They went back to their own village.
   - Ⓑ They fell over the cliff in the land of water.
   - Ⓒ They died of a strange fever.
   - Ⓓ They were attacked by bad strangers.

10. **On a separate sheet of paper, write an essay in response to the question below.**
    How does Sees Behind Trees change from the beginning to the end of the book?

Baseball in the Barrios

by Henry Horenstein

Reading Level

▶ Theme Connection

The young narrator of *Baseball in the Barrios* loves baseball. He and his friends have been playing organized baseball together in their homeland, Venezuela, since the age of four.

▶ Summary

Ten-year-old Hubaldo Antonio Romero Páez shares his love of, and experiences with, the game of béisbol. Although the Venezuelan setting and culture make the game a little different for Hubaldo than for young players in the United States, the fundamentals of the game, as well as the passion of the players, are shown to be universal.

▶ Building Background

Tell students that while baseball is often called the national pastime of the United States, they will be reading about a baseball player in another part of the world. Explain that *Baseball in the Barrios* is an informational narrative told from the point of view of a ten-year-old Venezuelan baseball enthusiast. Show the glossary at the end of the book, and point out that many of the words used in Spanish to talk about baseball are the same or almost the same as in English. Have students read to find out how the main character's experience with baseball is similar to, and different from, that of young players in the United States.

Author Profile

Photographer, author, artist, and teacher Henry Horenstein has more than two dozen books to his credit, including books for children as well as texts which are used in college photography and art classes. Horenstein spent two weeks with Hubaldo Romero Páez in Caracas, Venezuela, photographing *Baseball in the Barrios.*

Additional Books by the Author
- *Dog's Life*
- *How Is a Bicycle Made?*
- *Spring Training*

Vitabulary

Have students sort the vocabulary words into parts of speech using a chart like the following. See pages 158–161 for additional vocabulary activities.

Nouns	Verbs	Adjectives

Day 1
genius p. 4
prejudice p. 7
fielder p. 7

Day 2
formal p. 8
barrio p. 13
urban p. 13
fundamentals p. 14

Day 3
typical p. 16
regulation p. 19
legitimate p. 19
trespassers p. 19
currency p. 23

Day 4
budge p. 26
dugout p. 26
legendary p. 26

© Harcourt

	Response	Strategies	Skills
► Day 1 **Pages 1–7**	**Book Talk** • Characters' Traits • Main Idea • Important Details **Writing:** Make Predictions	**MAKE AND CONFIRM PREDICTIONS** `FOCUS STRATEGY`	**SUMMARIZE AND PARAPHRASE** `FOCUS SKILL` *Distant Voyages* pp. T182–T183
► Day 2 **Pages 8–15**	**Book Talk** • Author's Craft • Cause-Effect • Summarize **Writing:** Personal Narrative	Use Context to Confirm Meaning	Characterization *Distant Voyages* pp. T511A–T511B
► Day 3 **Pages 16–23**	**Book Talk** • Summarize • Cause-Effect • Compare and Contrast **Writing:** Express Personal Opinions	Create Mental Images	Draw Conclusions *Distant Voyages* pp. T160–T161
► Day 4 **Pages 24–27**	**Book Talk** • Make Connections • Theme • Compare and Contrast **Writing:** Express Personal Opinions	**MAKE AND CONFIRM PREDICTIONS** `FOCUS STRATEGY`	**SUMMARIZE AND PARAPHRASE** `FOCUS SKILL` *Distant Voyages* pp. T182–T183
► Day 5 **Wrap-Up**	**Project** ✓ Make a Baseball Map of the World • Inquiry Project **Writing** ✓ News Story **Language Link** • Specialized Terms **Assessment** ✓ Comprehension Test		

*Additional support is provided in *Trophies*.
✓ Options for Assessment

Baseball in the Barrios

BOOK TALK

After you read pages 1–7, meet with your group to discuss and respond to the following questions or statements:

1 Describe Hubaldo, including his interests and talents.

2 What does Hubaldo mean when he calls baseball an *all*-American game?

3 According to Hubaldo, why are there many more Latin American baseball players in the North American leagues today than there were before the 1950s?

Strategies Good Readers Use

FOCUS STRATEGY MAKE AND CONFIRM PREDICTIONS

*M*ake a prediction about what Hubaldo will do to work toward his goal of becoming a professional baseball player.

RESPONSE JOURNAL

Hubaldo has a big dream and a serious goal: to become a professional baseball player. Predict whether Hubaldo will reach his goal. Explain your reasoning.

SKILLS IN CONTEXT

FOCUS SKILL SUMMARIZE AND PARAPHRASE: WISH YOU WERE HERE! To summarize, you tell briefly the main idea and important details of a passage. To paraphrase, you restate a passage in your own words without changing the meaning. Imagine that you are Hubaldo and write a postcard to a friend in the United States. Describe your experiences in the book so far.

What You Need

- notebook paper
- writing and drawing materials
- index cards

Greetings from....

What to Do

1. Revisit pages 1–7 of *Baseball in the Barrios* to review Hubaldo's experiences. Make notes about the most important events.

2. Circle the event or events that you will include in a postcard.

3. On one side of the index card, write a message that Hubaldo might have written to a friend in the United States. Tell only the main ideas and important details about Hubaldo's experiences. Answer *who, what, where, when, why,* and how questions.

4. On the other side of the index card, draw a picture that shows an event from the story.

5. "Mail" your postcard to a classmate, or display it.

Here is a story event to help you get started: Carlos hit a home run to win the game.

Think Ahead
What do you think Hubaldo's daily life is like?

© Harcourt

Baseball in the Barrios

BOOK TALK

After you read pages 8–15, meet with your group to discuss and answer the following questions:

1 How does Hubaldo use his own experience to support the statement, "To be a good ballplayer, you must start early"?

2 Why might Hubaldo have a special respect for the major league baseball players Chico Carrasquel and Luis Aparicio?

3 In what ways do Hubaldo's parents support his interest in baseball?

RESPONSE JOURNAL

Imagine that you, like Hubaldo, are playing baseball in a stadium with three hundred cheering and shouting spectators. Write about how it feels to play before such a large crowd.

Strategies Good Readers Use

USE CONTEXT TO CONFIRM MEANING

Good readers use surrounding text to help figure out the meaning of unfamiliar words. Find some Spanish words—for example, *madrina*—in the text and see if you can figure out the meaning by using context clues.

SKILLS IN CONTEXT

CHARACTERIZATION: CHARACTER TRAIT MOBILE In *Baseball in the Barrios*, author Henry Horenstein tells the story of Hubaldo, using information Hubaldo has shared about himself. Authors provide information and details to develop characters in order to "bring them to life." Careful reading can reveal a lot about Hubaldo's character. Make a mobile that illustrates Hubaldo's character traits. You can add to it when you complete the book.

What You Need

- index cards
- construction paper
- tape and/or glue
- scissors
- markers
- string or yarn
- stapler

What to Do

1. Draw a picture of Hubaldo.

2. Think of adjectives that describe Hubaldo, and write them on small pieces of construction paper. Glue them onto index cards.

3. Use string to hang index cards one below the other from the picture of Hubaldo.

4. Hang up your mobile.

Here is an adjective to get you started: confident

confident

Think Ahead How might Hubaldo's practices compare to practices where you live?

© Harcourt

Baseball in the Barrios

BOOK TALK

After you read pages 16–23, meet with your group to discuss and respond to the following questions or statements:

1 Name some places where *caimanera* might be played in and around Caracas.

2 According to Hubaldo, what helps Latin ballplayers to become such good hitters? Why?

3 How were Simón Bolívar and George Washington alike and different?

RESPONSE JOURNAL

Do you think that practicing with planks of wood for bats and socks, rags, crushed juice containers, and cabbages for balls can make Hubaldo and his friends better ballplayers? Why or why not?

> ### Strategies Good Readers Use
>
> **CREATE MENTAL IMAGES**
>
> Review what you know about Hubaldo's baseball games in Caracas. Think about his neighborhood, playing field, spectators, and climate. In your mind, create a picture of one of Hubaldo's games.

SKILLS IN CONTEXT

DRAW CONCLUSIONS: GREAT GENERALIZATIONS Use statements from the text plus your own experience to draw conclusions while you read. After gathering this evidence, interpret it to make a generalization. Make a poster that illustrates the difference between a statement from the text and a generalization.

What You Need

- one sheet of construction paper
- self-stick notes
- pencils and markers
- list of statements (below)

Statements

- **Venezuelan kids play baseball on basketball courts, pavement, and farms.**
- **Planks of wood make great bats; socks, rags, and even cabbages can substitute for balls in Caracas.**

What to Do

1. Label the construction paper *Great Generalizations*.

2. Copy each statement below onto a self-stick note. Arrange the notes on the construction paper.

3. Under each note, write a generalization based on the statement and your knowledge and experience.

4. Exchange papers with a partner. Compare your partner's generalizations to the ones you made.

Here is an example to get you started:
Our field seats three hundred people, and on game nights it is packed. Generalization: *Baseball is extremely popular in Caracas.*

Think Ahead
What else might Hubaldo and his friends like to do?

© Harcourt

Baseball in the Barrios

BOOK TALK

After you read pages 24–27, meet with your group to discuss and respond to the following questions or statements:

1 What characters from selections in *Distant Voyages* remind you of Hubaldo? Explain.

2 What are some themes in *Baseball in the Barrios*?

3 Hubaldo's goal is to become a professional baseball player. Write about one of your goals, and compare and contrast it with Hubaldo's goal.

RESPONSE JOURNAL

Hubaldo's friends Romni and Rodni are important to him. Would you enjoy being friends with Hubaldo? Why?

Strategies Good Readers Use

FOCUS STRATEGY **MAKE AND CONFIRM PREDICTIONS**

Good readers make predictions and confirm or revise them as they read. Review the predictions you made while reading this book, and reflect on which predictions were confirmed and which you later revised.

SKILLS IN CONTEXT

FOCUS SKILL **SUMMARIZE AND PARAPHRASE: MAKE A PAMPHLET** When you summarize, you tell a shortened version of the original text. When you paraphrase, you restate the passage in your own words. Using information from *Baseball in the Barrios*, write a pamphlet summarizing and paraphrasing what you learned about baseball in Venezuela.

What You Need

- **notebook paper**
- **construction paper**
- **writing materials**

What to Do

1. Revisit *Baseball in the Barrios*. Summarize the story events, telling what it is like to play baseball in Venezuela.

2. Paraphrase one of the quotes or events in the story.

3. Fold a sheet of construction paper into a pamphlet. On the inside, use the head *Summary* and insert your summary of the two pages. On the opposite side, use the head *Paraphrase* and insert your paraphrase of the paragraph. Give your pamphlet a title.

4. Share your pamphlet with a classmate. Compare your summary and paraphrase, and note any important details.

Here is an important detail to get you started:
One of the most popular forms of baseball in Venezuela is called chapitas.

Wrap-Up

▶ **Project** MAKE A BASEBALL MAP OF THE WORLD Remind students that in *Baseball in the Barrios*, Hubaldo proudly points out that baseball has been played in Venezuela almost as long as in the United States. He also mentions several other countries where the sport is played. Have students work in groups to create world maps that show where baseball is played. Ask students to complete the copying master on page 47 to plan their maps. Then have each group create and present their map.

▶ **Writing** NEWS STORY Have students respond to the following prompt: **Imagine that you are a news reporter for the Caracas newspaper *El Nacional*. Write an informative newspaper story about one of Hubaldo's games.** Have students use the copying master on page 48 to plan their story. Rubrics for evaluating student writing can be found on pages 154–157.

▶ **Language Link** SPECIALIZED TERMS Many sports, jobs, and other activities have special vocabulary. Have students make a list of baseball terms, such as *bunt* and *foul*, and have them use a dictionary to define the terms.

Inquiry Project

Baseball in the Barrios provides a personal introduction to one child's life in Venezuela. Have students fill in a K-W-L chart about Venezuela. Have students first list things they know or think they know about the country. Next, have them list things they would like to find out. Then have them use reference books and the Internet to research the answers to their questions.

K What I Know	W What I Want to Know	L What I Learned

✔ **Comprehension Test** Test students' comprehension of *Baseball in the Barrios* by having them complete the copying master on page 49.

Name _____

Project Planner

In *Baseball in the Barrios*, Hubaldo proudly points out that baseball, or *béisbol*, has been played in Venezuela almost as long as it has been played in the United States. He also mentions several other countries where the sport is played. With your group, create a world map that shows countries and continents where baseball is played.

What You Need

- white paper or tracing paper
- pencil and colored pencils or markers
- research materials (*World Almanac*, atlas, encyclopedia, the Internet)

☐ **Step 1.** Review with your group *Baseball in the Barrios* to find all countries mentioned by Hubaldo. Check reference sources to discover other countries where baseball is played. Make a list of these countries.

_____

_____

_____   _____

_____   _____

_____   _____

☐ **Step 2.** On a separate sheet of paper, make a graphic organizer like the one below. Use the graphic organizer to sort countries by continent.

North America	South America	Africa	Europe	Asia	Australia	Antarctica

☐ **Step 3.** Trace a world map, either from the back of *Baseball in the Barrios* or from an atlas, and label each continent.

☐ **Step 4.** Write names of all baseball-playing countries around the world. Draw lines from each country name to its location.

☐ **Step 5.** As a group, present your map to the class.

News Story

Imagine that you are a news reporter for the Caracas newspaper *El Nacional*. Write an
informative newspaper story about one of Hubaldo's games. Complete the organizer below to plan your
story. Then write your story.

Prewriting Graphic Organizer

WHO is playing:

Team 1: _____

Team 2: _____

WHEN is the game:

Date: _____

Time: _____

WHERE is the game: _____

WHAT happens:

First exciting play: _____

_____

Second exciting play: _____

_____

Third exciting play: _____

_____

© Harcourt

Name _____

Comprehension Test   Test Prep

Read each question below. Then mark the letter for the answer you have chosen.

1. **Why does Hubaldo dream about winning the national championship?**
   - Ⓐ He wants to please his parents.
   - Ⓑ His best friend is on the other team.
   - Ⓒ His goal is to become a professional baseball player.
   - Ⓓ His mother is the team's godmother.

2. **Why does Hubaldo say that he is a good fielder?**
   - Ⓕ He leads the league in home runs.
   - Ⓖ Very few ground balls get past him.
   - Ⓗ He brags a lot and likes to show off.
   - Ⓙ He plays well on pavement.

3. **Why is *chapitas* a popular game in Venezuela?**
   - Ⓐ There are a lot of bottle caps in the cities.
   - Ⓑ Children do not have balls in Venezuela.
   - Ⓒ It is challenging to hit small bottle caps.
   - Ⓓ Bottle caps do not break windows.

4. **Why can Hubaldo play baseball all year?**
   - Ⓕ He does not have much homework.
   - Ⓖ Baseball is the only sport played in the barrio where he lives.
   - Ⓗ There is always a well-maintained field available.
   - Ⓙ It is usually warm and sunny.

5. **Which word *best* describes Hubaldo?**
   - Ⓐ determined
   - Ⓑ lazy
   - Ⓒ shy
   - Ⓓ friendly

6. **In league games, ballplayers use—**
   - Ⓕ basketball courts.
   - Ⓖ normal bats and gloves.
   - Ⓗ *chapitas*.
   - Ⓙ rolled-up socks and planks of wood.

7. **What is the idea behind the *Semillitas*, or "little seeds"?**
   - Ⓐ Young players will grow into older, skilled ballplayers.
   - Ⓑ They are the children of famous ballplayers.
   - Ⓒ Newspapers print photos of young players.
   - Ⓓ They are popular with the fans.

8. **Why is Simón Bolívar Venezuela's greatest national hero ?**
   - Ⓕ He is a great shortstop.
   - Ⓖ His picture is on the currency.
   - Ⓗ He freed Venezuela from Spanish rule.
   - Ⓙ He helped George Washington.

9. **Why does Hubaldo say "We don't really need a field"?**
   - Ⓐ There are no regulation fields in the barrio.
   - Ⓑ Fields are often not mowed anyway.
   - Ⓒ He prefers playing on pavement.
   - Ⓓ Informal games can be played anywhere.

10. **On a separate sheet of paper, write a short answer in response to this question:**
   Will Hubaldo achieve his goal? Use evidence from the story to support your answer.

The Tarantula in My Purse

Reading Level

by Jean Craighead George

▶ Theme Connection

As students read *The Tarantula in My Purse*, they will have a greater understanding of how humans and animals can work together to their mutual benefit. They will also see how the author's personal experiences with wild animals has provided her with background for her books.

▶ Summary

With humor and loving pride, author-naturalist Jean Craighead George relates a series of vignettes about the wild creatures—including crows, ducks, snakes, bats, raccoons, and the title tarantula—that she and her three growing children rescued, nurtured, and eventually released back into the wild.

▶ Building Background

Survey the class to find out what kinds of pets students have or have had. Ask them to identify the most unusual pets on the list. Then explain that they will be reading *The Tarantula in My Purse*, an informational narrative about living with an assortment of unusual wild animal pets. Have them read to find out what the author and her family learned from sharing their lives with wild creatures.

Author Profile

"Children are still in love with the wonders of nature, and I am too," writes award-winning author Jean Craighead George. Born into a family of naturalists, George admits that her list of more than sixty children's titles is "enough to scare off even me." Among her many popular books is *Julie of the Wolves*, which won the Newbery medal in 1973.

Additional Books by the Author
- *The Cry of the Crow*
- *My Side of the Mountain*

Vocabulary

Help students relate new vocabulary to background knowledge about animals. Ask them to complete a chart like the one below by using vocabulary words in phrases that describe various animals. Have them underline vocabulary words in the phrases. See pages 158–161 for additional vocabulary activities.

Wild Animal Words

Turkey Vulture	Screech Owl	Kestrel
young covered with fluffy white down	preening feathers	soars on thermals
chicks are gawky		young called fledglings

Day 1
gawky p. 3
primordial p. 5
preening p. 9

Day 2
gluttonous p. 46
aggressive p. 48
formula p. 61
comeuppance p. 64

Day 3
thermals p. 73
fledgling p. 84
abduct p. 92
docile p. 96

Day 4
dormancy p. 110
extricated p. 116
coveys p. 124

© Harcourt

	Response	Strategies	Skills
Day 1 Pages 1–36	**Book Talk** • Draw Conclusions • Important Details • Cause-Effect **Writing:** React to Story	**SUMMARIZE** FOCUS STRATEGY	**DRAW CONCLUSIONS** FOCUS SKILL *Distant Voyages pp. T160–T161
Day 2 Pages 37–72	**Book Talk** • Important Details • Important Details • Draw Conclusions **Writing:** Problem Solving	Create Mental Images	Text Structure: Main Idea and Details *Distant Voyages pp. T318–T319
Day 3 Pages 73–101	**Book Talk** • Draw Conclusions • Characters' Emotions • Cause-Effect **Writing:** Identify with Characters	Create Mental Images	Text Structure: Main Idea and Details *Distant Voyages pp. T318–T319
Day 4 Pages 102–134	**Book Talk** • Make Comparisons • Theme • Express Personal Opinion **Writing:** Personal Response	**SUMMARIZE** FOCUS STRATEGY	**DRAW CONCLUSIONS** FOCUS SKILL *Distant Voyages pp. T160–T161
Day 5 Wrap-Up	**Project** ✓ Create a How-To Booklet • Inquiry Project **Writing** ✓ Personal Narrative **Language Link** • Vivid Language **Assessment** ✓ Comprehension Test		

*Additional support is provided in *Trophies*.
✓ Options for Assessment

The Tarantula in My Purse

BOOK TALK

After you read pages 1–36, meet with your group to discuss and answer the following questions:

1 How do you think the author's childhood might have influenced her as she raised her own children?

2 What was unusual about Yammer the screech owl?

3 How did imprinting affect the goose and the duck?

RESPONSE JOURNAL

How did you feel when Yammer flew off and never returned? Write a journal entry that explains your reaction. Be sure to use referents and clear antecedents in your writing.

> **Strategies Good Readers Use**
>
> **FOCUS STRATEGY SUMMARIZE**
>
> Good readers summarize important points and put them into their own words. Write a short summary about the Georges' experience with one animal.

SKILLS IN CONTEXT

FOCUS SKILL DRAW CONCLUSIONS: CONCLUSION CHALLENGE A conclusion is a statement that is likely to be true based on information found in the text and/or your own personal experience. Challenge your classmates to draw conclusions about what you have read so far in *The Tarantula in My Purse*.

What You Need

- index cards
- pen or pencil

What to Do

1. Skim *The Tarantula in My Purse*. On separate index cards, write questions about what you have read. Ask *why* and *how* questions that take some thought and that are not directly answered in the text.

2. The class will work as two teams. Take turns asking your questions to the opposing team.

3. For every correct or logical conclusion, the answering team receives one point.

4. The team with the most points wins.

Here's a question to get you started:
How does the author feel about animals?

Think Ahead
What other unusual pets do you think the George family will adopt?

© Harcourt

The Tarantula in My Purse

Day 2   Pages 37–72

BOOK TALK

After you read pages 37–72, meet with your group to discuss and respond to the following questions or statements:

1 Why did the author think Hilde must have kicked or hurt New York?

2 List evidence the author gives to support this statement: "Crows are intelligent animals."

3 What did Luke mean when he said "Crayfish have to live"?

Strategies Good Readers Use

CREATE MENTAL IMAGES

Create a mental image of one of the scenes on pages 37–72. How does this strategy help you better understand the story?

RESPONSE JOURNAL

Think about the Georges' experience with the animals in the indoor pool. Write a journal entry that describes how you would have tried to solve the mystery.

SKILLS IN CONTEXT

TEXT STRUCTURE: MAIN IDEA AND DETAILS: QUESTION AND ANSWER WHEEL Good notes summarize and record only the main ideas in what you read. Use *The Tarantula in My Purse* as a reference and take notes about the main ideas in the book. Then turn your notes into a Question and Answer Wheel. Use the wheel to review what you learned or to quiz someone else.

What You Need

- **two sheets of light-colored construction paper**
- **compasses**
- **ruler**
- **scissors**
- **round-headed paper fastener**
- **pencil, pen, or fine-line marker**

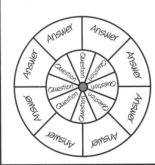

What to Do

1. Use the compasses to draw an 8-inch circle on one sheet of paper and a 4-inch circle on the other. Draw lines to divide each circle into eight equal wedges. Then cut out both circles. Place the smaller circle on the larger one and attach at the center.

2. Identify eight main ideas that you learned from the book. Turn each fact into a question and write it in a space on the smaller circle. Number the spaces from 1 to 8.

3. Write the answer to each question in one of the spaces on the larger circle. On the back, write the matching question number.

4. Invite someone to turn the wheel to match a question to its answer.

Here are a question and an answer to get you started: *Q: Why is a crow hard to study? A: Crows are very smart.*

Think Ahead What future problems do you think Crowbar might cause for the Georges?

© Harcourt

The Tarantula in My Purse • **53**

The Tarantula in My Purse

BOOK TALK

After you read pages 73–101, meet with your group to discuss and answer the following questions:

1 Why did the author usually tell people to take baby robins back where they had been found?

2 How did Luke's attitude toward wild animals differ from the attitudes of Twig and Craig?

3 Why did Crowbar leave the Georges?

RESPONSE JOURNAL

Imagine that you are part of the George family. Write a journal entry describing your feelings when Crowbar flies away for good.

> ### Strategies Good Readers Use
>
> #### CREATE MENTAL IMAGES
>
> Think about one of the events you read about in pages 73–101. Then close your eyes and form a mental image of the event. Draw a picture to share your image with another reader.

SKILLS IN CONTEXT

TEXT STRUCTURE: MAIN IDEA AND DETAILS: MAIN IDEA MOBILE A paragraph or a group of paragraphs usually has one main idea. The rest of that section of text includes details that support that idea. Make a mobile that illustrates the main idea and details of a selection from *The Tarantula in My Purse*. A roomful of main idea mobiles can provide you and your classmates with a quick review of what you have read!

What You Need

- **12" x 3" piece of poster board**
- **index cards**
- **pencil**
- **hole punch**
- **string**
- **drawing tools**

What to Do

1. Choose a text selection that interests you. Identify the main idea and several supporting details.

2. Write a main idea sentence on one side of the 12" x 3" piece of poster board. On the other side, draw a picture to accompany your sentence.

3. Write each supporting detail on a separate index card. Add a picture or symbol on the opposite side.

4. Punch a hole at the center top of the main idea poster board and attach a loop of string as a hanger. Punch holes along the bottom and attach each detail card. Then hang up your mobile.

Here is a main idea to get you started:

The baby robin wanted to eat constantly. (page 82)

Think Ahead
Do you think Crowbar will come back to visit or to stay? Explain.

The Tarantula in My Purse

BOOK TALK

After you read pages 102–134, meet with your group to discuss and answer the following questions:

1 What selections in *Distant Voyages* remind you of *The Tarantula in My Purse*? Explain.

2 What do you think is the most important lesson Twig, Craig, and Luke learned from growing up with wild animals in their home?

3 Of all the animals described in the book, which would you most like to live with? Why?

Strategies Good Readers Use

FOCUS STRATEGY **SUMMARIZE**

*L*ist the main events that occur in one chapter in pages 102–134 of *The Tarantula in My Purse*. Use your list to write a summary of the chapter.

RESPONSE JOURNAL

Think about the scene where Boay eats a rat or Twig's experiment with white mice. Write a journal entry that describes your feelings as you read about one of these events.

SKILLS IN CONTEXT

FOCUS SKILL **DRAW CONCLUSIONS: CONCLUSION EQUATIONS** To be able to draw a conclusion, you must use details in the book and your own knowledge and experience. Revisit pages 102–134 of *The Tarantula in My Purse* and find places where you had to draw conclusions. Then create Conclusion Equations to show what conclusions you made and how you made them.

What You Need

- index cards
- writing tools

What to Do

1. Revisit pages 102–134 to find places where you drew conclusions using details from the book and your own knowledge.

2. Choose three conclusions. For each conclusion, write the details the author gave you on one card and what you already knew on another card. Write the conclusions on a third card.

3. Draw a plus sign on one card and an equal sign on another card.

4. Trade equations with a partner, and see if you can solve each other's equations by putting the cards in the right order.

Here's a conclusion to get you started:
Twig, Luke, and Craig respect wild animals.

© Harcourt

Wrap-Up

▶ **Project** **CREATE A HOW-TO BOOKLET** Remind students that Jean Craighead George, author of *The Tarantula in My Purse*, fills her narrative with facts and observations about how to care for wild animals. Tell students they will be creating how-to booklets to share information about caring for a pet or a wild animal.
- Organize students into groups.
- Ask each group to complete the copying master on page 57 to plan the information they want to include.
- Then have groups create their booklets.
- Invite groups to share their booklets.

▶ **Writing** **PERSONAL NARRATIVE** Have students respond to the following writing prompt: **Describe one of your most memorable experiences with a pet or a wild animal.** Have students use the copying master on page 58 to plan their paragraphs. Remind students to work at their writing voice. Rubrics for evaluating student writing are provided on pages 154–157.

▶ **Language Link** **VIVID LANGUAGE** The author uses colorful language to describe the wild animals she and her family raise. Have students list several examples of descriptions they find especially appealing.

Inquiry Project

The Tarantula in My Purse can be a springboard for inquiry into a variety of animal topics. Have students brainstorm topics they would like to know more about. Invite them to use reference books, the Internet, and CD-ROMs to find information on their topics.

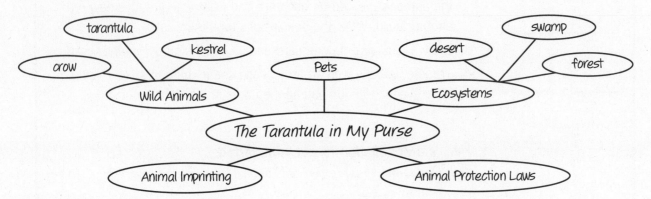

✔ **Comprehension Test** Test students' comprehension of *The Tarantula in My Purse* by having them complete the copying master on page 59.

Name _____

Project Planner

Jean Craighead George used reference materials to help her find out how to meet the needs of wild animals that she and her family adopted. With your group, create a helpful how-to booklet that shares what you learn about caring for one kind of animal. The animal can be either wild or a pet. Use the form below to plan your project.

☐ **Step 1.** Brainstorm a list of wild animals and/or pets that a person might need to care for. Record your group's choice here:

_____

What You Need

- paper
- writing and drawing materials
- additional references (books, the Internet, CD-ROMs, etc.)

☐ **Step 2.** Look through the book and other references to get ideas about what should be included in the booklet. For example, what does the animal eat? Use this information to help you decide upon sections for your booklet. Then list each section topic in one of the ovals on the web below. (Add more ovals if you plan to have more than four sections.) Decide which reference sources you will use to find information on each topic.

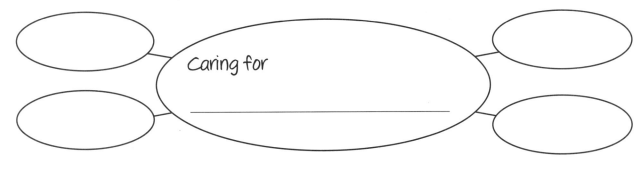

Caring for
_____

☐ **Step 3.** Work together to research and write each section of the how-to booklet. You can create your booklet with a word processing program or by writing on paper. Add illustrations, staple your pages together, and create a cover for your booklet.

☐ **Step 4.** As a group, summarize the information in your booklet by giving a short presentation about how to care for your animal.

Feeding a Baby Robin

© Harcourt

Name _____

Personal Narrative

Write a personal narrative that tells about your most memorable experience with a pet or a wild animal. Complete the graphic organizer below to plan your narrative.

Prewriting Graphic Organizer

Introduction: How and when did you find or get this animal?

_____

What Happened?

Event: _____

_____

Event: _____

_____

Event: _____

_____

Conclusion: Why was your experience memorable? What did you learn? How did the experience change you?

_____

_____

_____

Name _____

Comprehension Test

Read each question below. Then mark the letter for the answer you have chosen.

1. **Why did Yammer the owl like Craig's train?**
   - Ⓐ The train wrecks were exciting.
   - Ⓑ The whistle sounded like a mother owl.
   - Ⓒ The engine was the same size as a mouse.
   - Ⓓ The train moved like a snake.

2. **Why did the Georges take the baby wood ducks to a pond?**
   - Ⓕ The ducks were eating too much.
   - Ⓖ They hoped a mallard would adopt them.
   - Ⓗ The ducks had been born near the pond.
   - Ⓙ It was illegal to keep the ducks.

3. **Why was Crowbar more imprinted on humans than New York had been?**
   - Ⓐ Crowbar was younger when he was adopted.
   - Ⓑ Crowbar slept inside and New York didn't.
   - Ⓒ The Georges fed Crowbar more.
   - Ⓓ Crowbar was smarter than New York.

4. **Which of the following is evidence of Crowbar's intelligence?**
   - Ⓕ He ate hamburger.
   - Ⓖ He pushed mugs back after stealing.
   - Ⓗ He was not afraid of other birds.
   - Ⓙ He stole shiny objects.

5. **Why was the author worried when Iliad the kestrel escaped?**
   - Ⓐ The kestrel would eat all the songbirds.
   - Ⓑ The bird was too young to live on its own.
   - Ⓒ Crowbar might fly off after the kestrel.
   - Ⓓ The ring on his foot could trap him.

6. **Why didn't the Georges worry about being sprayed by Mason the skunk?**
   - Ⓕ Mason's scent gland had been removed.
   - Ⓖ Skunks never spray people who feed them.
   - Ⓗ Skunks spray only when threatened.
   - Ⓙ Mason was waving his tail in the air.

7. **After putting the tarantula inside, why did the author handle the purse carefully?**
   - Ⓐ A tarantula's outer covering is very fragile.
   - Ⓑ Tarantulas are very dangerous spiders.
   - Ⓒ She was afraid the tarantula would bite her.
   - Ⓓ The tarantula was carrying an egg sac.

8. **Why was the author worried when a sparrow nested in a guest's tie?**
   - Ⓕ The guest was afraid of birds.
   - Ⓖ She was afraid the sparrow was in danger.
   - Ⓗ She knew the bird would not want to leave.
   - Ⓙ The sparrow did not have enough room.

9. **Why was Rana the bullfrog the author's all-time favorite pet?**
   - Ⓐ Craig had given her the bullfrog.
   - Ⓑ The bullfrog chased off a young man she did not like.
   - Ⓒ She liked to listen to the bullfrog's song.
   - Ⓓ The bullfrog kept the house free of insects.

10. **On a separate sheet of paper, write a short answer in response to the question below.**
    Should people be encouraged to raise wild animals in their homes? Explain your answer.

© Harcourt

Maria's Comet

by Deborah Hopkinson

Reading Level

▶ Theme Connection

As students read *Maria's Comet*, they will learn about events that took place during the childhood of Maria Mitchell, whose early fervent interest in astronomy led her to become America's first female astronomer. *Maria's Comet* presents and develops the themes of space exploration and our quest for growth and change.

▶ Summary

Young Maria Mitchell, who eventually becomes America's first female astronomer, yearns to assist her father in his rooftop observatory. Fervent in her desire to explore the stars, she must overcome nineteenth-century attitudes about the accepted roles of young women.

▶ Building Background

Tell students that *Maria's Comet* is an example of historical fiction. The story is set in the past, and it features real people and events. Point out that historians often know very few facts about the childhoods of famous people.

Therefore, authors of historical fiction attempt to create realistic stories and situations, using fiction to "fill in the blanks" between established facts. Have students read *Maria's Comet* to find out the experiences that ultimately led Maria Mitchell to become a famous astronomer.

Author Profile

Deborah Hopkinson has received critical acclaim and prestigious awards for her four children's books, including the Parents' Choice Silver Honor and the International Reading Association award. In all her books, Hopkinson presents strong young female characters who are committed to reaching ambitious, and often heroic, goals.

Additional Books by the Author

- *Birdie's Lighthouse*
- *Sweet Clara and the Freedom Quilt*
- *A Band of Angels*

Vocabulary

Have students print each of the vocabulary words on an index card. Then have them work together to sort the words into such categories as words that name objects, name careers, describe actions, describe objects, or have multiple-meanings. Then have students take turns using the words in original sentences. See pages 158–161 for additional vocabulary activities.

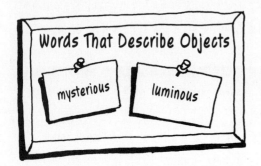

Words That Describe Objects
mysterious   luminous

Day 1	Day 2	Day 3	Day 4
shimmering p. 3	comets p. 7	harbor p. 14	luminous p. 22
astronomer p. 4	mysterious p. 7	journey p. 20	constellation p. 22
telescope p. 4	anchor p. 10		gleams p. 26
fiercely p. 4	yarns p. 12		

	Response	Strategies	Skills
Day 1 Pages 1–5	**Book Talk** • Compare and Contrast • Imagery • Summarize **Writing:** Express Personal Opinions	**SELF-QUESTION** FOCUS STRATEGY	**TEXT STRUCTURE: MAIN IDEA AND DETAILS** FOCUS SKILL *Distant Voyages* pp. T318–T319
Day 2 Pages 6–13	**Book Talk** • Imagery • Summarize • Determine Characters' Emotions **Writing:** Express Personal Opinions	Summarize	Text Structure: Compare and Contrast *Distant Voyages* pp. T510–T511
Day 3 Pages 14–21	**Book Talk** • Compare and Contrast • Characters' Traits • Cause-Effect **Writing:** Identify with Characters	Use Context to Confirm Meaning	Narrative Elements *Distant Voyages* pp. T68–T69
Day 4 Pages 22–27	**Book Talk** • Imagery • Draw Conclusions • Make Comparisons **Writing:** Personal Response	**SELF-QUESTION** FOCUS STRATEGY	**TEXT STRUCTURE: MAIN IDEA AND DETAILS** FOCUS SKILL *Distant Voyages* pp. T318–T319

Day 5
Wrap-Up

Project
✓ Multimedia Presentation
• Inquiry Project

Writing
✓ Persuasive Essay

Language Link
• Vivid Verbs

Assessment
✓ Comprehension Test

*Additional support is provided in *Trophies*.
✓ Options for Assessment

Maria's Comet

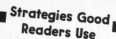

BOOK TALK

After you read pages 1–5, meet with your group to discuss and answer the following questions:

❶ When Maria was a little girl, what did she think her father did? How did her knowledge grow and change?

❷ According to Maria, how is an astronomer like a "sailor scanning the waves"?

❸ How does a telescope work?

RESPONSE JOURNAL

Do you enjoy looking at stars? Explain why or why not in your journal.

Strategies Good Readers Use

FOCUS STRATEGY SELF-QUESTION

☆On pages 1–5, Deborah Hopkinson uses many figures of speech to compare two things that might not seem similar, such as stars and specks of dust. To understand such comparisons, ask yourself, *How are these two things alike?*

SKILLS IN CONTEXT

FOCUS SKILL TEXT STRUCTURE: MAIN IDEA AND DETAILS: YOU ARE THE REPORTER Remembering the main events in a story helps you to better understand the story. Imagine that you are a newspaper reporter. Your job is to write a news flash—a short, quick report about the main idea of *Maria's Comet* so far.

What You Need

- paper
- writing and drawing tools

What to Do

1. Revisit the story and list the main events in order.

2. Write your news flash. Begin with a sentence that sums up the main idea of the story so far. Use details from the story to support your sentence.

3. Draw a picture to go with your news flash.

4. Present your news flash to a classmate as if you were a reporter on television.

Here is an idea for a way to begin your news flash: An astronomer shows his daughter how to find constellations through his telescope.

Think Ahead Does Maria's father encourage her to become interested in astronomy?

Maria's Comet

BOOK TALK

After you read pages 6–13, meet with your group to discuss and answer the following questions:

1 Why do Maria and her father consider comets "mysterious visitors"?

2 How many planets had been discovered at the time this story takes place? Which planets were discovered at a later time?

3 How do you think Maria feels about doing her chores while her father "sweeps the sky"?

RESPONSE JOURNAL

Would you enjoy going to the attic hideaway with Maria and Andrew? Why or why not?

SKILLS IN CONTEXT

TEXT STRUCTURE: COMPARE AND CONTRAST: COMPARE AND CONTRAST CHARACTERS   How are Maria and her brother Andrew similar? How are they different? Follow the steps below to compare and contrast them. Using information from *Maria's Comet*, show the similarities and differences between the ideas and interests of Maria and her brother Andrew.

What You Need

- pencil
- paper
- compass

What to Do

1. Create a Venn diagram. Use a compass to draw two large overlapping circles. Label the left circle *Maria*, the middle portion *Maria and Andrew*, and the right circle *Andrew*.

2. Review pages 12 and 13 of *Maria's Comet*. Then use the information to complete the diagram.

3. Compare your Venn diagram with a classmate's diagram, and discuss what you have learned.

Here is a comparison related to the interests of Andrew and Maria to get you started: Sailors and astronomers could both be classified as explorers.

Think Ahead

What might Andrew's interest in the sea lead him to do?

Maria's Comet

BOOK TALK

After you read pages 14–21, meet with your group
to discuss and answer the following questions:

1 How are Andrew's and Maria's goals similar and different?

2 How do you know that Maria is kind and strong?

3 What does Maria ask her father, and why is she afraid?

RESPONSE JOURNAL

Have you, like Maria, ever found that "sometimes
even a few steps can be as hard to take as a
journey to a distant land"? Explain.

Strategies Good Readers Use

USE CONTEXT TO CONFIRM MEANING

You can look for context clues that provide hints about the author's meaning. Use context—Maria's feelings and goals—to explain what she means when she says, "I turn his words over and over, like an otter trying to open an oyster shell."

SKILLS IN CONTEXT

NARRATIVE ELEMENTS: EXAMINE THE SETTING Review the portions of *Maria's Comet* that you
have read. What facts are provided or suggested about the time, the place, and widely held ideas
and attitudes? Use details in the text and illustrations to make a chart that examines the setting.

What You Need

- **chart paper**
- **pencil or drawing tools**

What to Do

1. Draw on chart paper a chart similar to the one below.
2. Use details provided and suggested by the text and illustrations of *Maria's Comet* to complete the chart.
3. Look at your chart, and draw conclusions about the setting. Support your conclusions with specific details from the story.
4. Discuss your conclusions with a classmate.

Place	Time	Ideas and Attitudes of Time

Here is a text detail to get you started:
*Maria fears that her parents will say that
"a girl should only look through the eye of a
sewing needle."*

Think Ahead
Will Maria's parents say
yes or no? Explain.

Maria's Comet

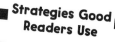

BOOK TALK

After you read pages 22–27, meet with your group to discuss and answer the following questions:

1 What mental image does the author create by having Maria compare the Milky Way to a "crazy, luminous quilt"?

2 Why does Maria think that Andrew might be looking at Polaris?

3 What characters in other selections you have read seem to share character traits with Maria?

RESPONSE JOURNAL

What interest, hobby, or goal might "light your heart" the way viewing a star through the telescope lit Maria's? Explain.

Strategies Good Readers Use

FOCUS STRATEGY **SELF-QUESTION**

*P*ages 22–24 contain many facts about stars and constellations. Write one or more questions that you asked yourself as you read. How did this strategy help you understand what you were reading?

SKILLS IN CONTEXT

FOCUS SKILL **TEXT STRUCTURE: MAIN IDEA AND DETAILS: A MATCHING ACTIVITY** Every paragraph has a main idea. Supporting details explain or give examples of the main idea. Play a game with another team in which you match main ideas with details. The team with the most matches wins.

What You Need

- index cards labeled *Main Idea*
- index cards labeled *Detail*
- markers

What to Do

1. With a partner, select the paragraphs from page 26.

2. Write the main idea and two supporting details from each paragraph on separate labeled cards.

3. Play a matching game with another team. Combine the cards. Give half the Main Idea cards and three Detail cards to each team. Place the remaining cards in a pile.

4. If a team has two details that match one main idea, put those cards aside. If not, draw a card from the pile to try to make a match. Teams take turns drawing cards and matching main ideas and details until all matches have been made.

Here is a text detail to get you started:
In 1865 Maria Mitchell was named the first professor of astronomy at Vassar College.

Wrap-Up

► Project

MULTIMEDIA PRESENTATION Gather resource materials and, if possible, films, film strips, and Internet interactive displays about comets, planets, stars, constellations, and the Milky Way. Display and discuss these materials.

- Organize students into groups, and assign each group a specific topic relating to space.
- Direct group members to research their topic and create a multimedia presentation.
- Ask students to complete the copying master on page 67 to help them plan their presentations.
- Have students present their projects to the class.

► Writing

PERSUASIVE ESSAY Have students write a persuasive essay to respond to the following writing prompt: **Write an essay that Maria might have written, in which she uses reasons, facts, and details to persuade her parents to let her go to school to learn to be an astronomer.** Have students use the copying master on page 68 to plan their essays. Remind students to focus on word choice. Rubrics for evaluating student writing are provided on pages 154–157.

► Language Link

VIVID VERBS Explain that vivid verbs give specific descriptions. As examples, use the verbs *race* and *tiptoe*. Contrast them with vague, general verbs, such as *go* and *walk*. Challenge students to list as many vivid verbs as they can find in *Maria's Comet*. Have students compare lists and take turns defining the vivid verbs and using them in original sentences.

Inquiry Project

Maria's Comet can be a springboard for inquiry into a variety of topics and ideas. Have students brainstorm topics they would like to know more about and organize their responses in a web. Students can use reference books and the Internet to begin their inquiry projects.

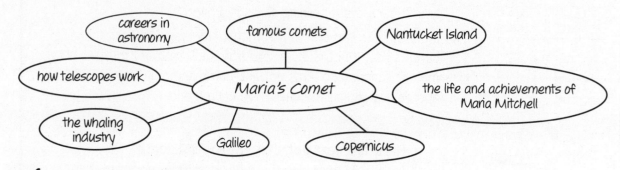

✔ Comprehension Test

Test students' comprehension of *Maria's Comet* by having them complete the copying master on page 69.

Name _____

Project Planner

Work together with your group members to plan, research, and create a multimedia presentation on the topic assigned by your teacher.

☐ **Step 1.** Use the web below to help you plan your project. Write your group's topic in the center oval. Use the outer ovals to brainstorm ideas about how to develop the topic into an interesting project. Include both written and visual materials (such as murals, mobiles, charts, or diagrams) in your project plans.

What You Need

- board or large sheet of newsprint
- research materials
- writing and drawing materials
- word processing and graphics software

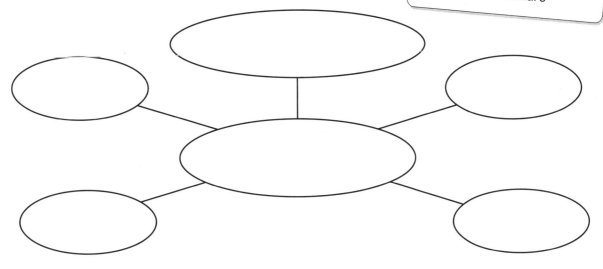

☐ **Step 2.** Work together to select the best ideas on your web. Then break the project down so that each group member is responsible for developing an equal part of it. Decide what materials each member will need and how such materials can be gathered.

☐ **Step 3.** Each group member should work independently on his or her part of the project. Agree on a time by which members must have completed their tasks. Then agree on a time to meet again as a group.

☐ **Step 4.** At the follow-up meeting, discuss each member's contribution. Organize the final materials, and rehearse the oral portions of your presentation.

☐ **Step 5.** As a group, present your project to the class.

© Harcourt

Persuasive Essay

Write an essay that Maria might have written, in which she uses reasons, facts, and details to persuade her parents to let her go to school to learn to be an astronomer. Complete the graphic organizer below to plan your essay.

Prewriting Graphic Organizer

Topic: _____

Audience: _____

Opinion Clearly Stated: _____

Reason 1: _____

Details: _____

Reason 2: _____

Details: _____

Reason 3: _____

Details: _____

Opinion Restated: _____

Action Requested: _____

Name _____

Comprehension Test

Read each question below. Then circle the letter for the answer you have chosen.

1. **What does Maria's father do every night as darkness falls?**
   - Ⓐ He helps wash the dishes.
   - Ⓑ He goes to the roof to play his guitar.
   - Ⓒ He goes to the roof to use his telescope.
   - Ⓓ He goes to the basement to fix his telescope.

2. **What bodies in space have "blurry heads and glowing tails"?**
   - Ⓕ stars
   - Ⓖ comets
   - Ⓗ constellations
   - Ⓙ planets

3. **What are some of Maria's chores?**
   - Ⓐ helping her father write his books
   - Ⓑ sweeping, mending, and taking care of her brothers and sisters
   - Ⓒ cleaning and painting her uncle's whaling boat
   - Ⓓ writing letters to Andrew and shoveling snow

4. **How are Maria and Andrew alike?**
   - Ⓕ They both want to be explorers.
   - Ⓖ They both want to go to sea.
   - Ⓗ They both love stories about sailors.
   - Ⓙ They both want to leave Nantucket Island.

5. **What happens to Andrew?**
   - Ⓐ He is injured on the roof.
   - Ⓑ He goes away on a whaling ship.
   - Ⓒ He discovers a comet.
   - Ⓓ He is the first person to see Polaris.

6. **What does Maria ask her father?**
   - Ⓕ to let her travel with Andrew
   - Ⓖ to let her write to Andrew
   - Ⓗ to let her go with him to the roof
   - Ⓙ to let her open the sea chest

7. **What are Orion the Hunter and Taurus the Bull?**
   - Ⓐ characters in one of Maria's books
   - Ⓑ the names of comets
   - Ⓒ the names of whaling ships
   - Ⓓ the names of constellations

8. **How does Polaris help sailors find their way?**
   - Ⓕ It has a tail like an arrow.
   - Ⓖ It is always north.
   - Ⓗ It is a red star.
   - Ⓙ It is part of a constellation that points to shore.

9. **What does Maria mean when she says that the star "lights her heart"?**
   - Ⓐ It burns like a very hot fire.
   - Ⓑ It scares her.
   - Ⓒ It makes her excited and happy.
   - Ⓓ It is so bright that it hurts to look at it.

10. **On a separate sheet of paper, write a short answer in response to the question below.**

    Which would you enjoy more: exploring the world on a whaling ship or exploring the stars through a telescope? Explain.

© Harcourt

Stone Wall Secrets

Reading Level

by Kristine and Robert Thorson

> ### ► Theme Connection
> *Stone Wall Secrets* spotlights planet Earth—a mysterious, fascinating, changing planet.

Author Profile
Kristine and Robert Thorson collaborated to write *Stone Wall Secrets*. Kristine Thorson has been a teacher, social worker, and cook in the Alaska wilderness. Robert Thorson is a professor of geology and geophysics at the University of Connecticut.

> ### ► Summary
> When Adam's grandfather receives a letter offering him money for the stones that form the walls around his New England homestead, he shares with Adam parts of the geologic and natural history of his farm. As he does so, it becomes as clear to Adam as it is to his grandfather that the rocks are an integral and priceless part of Adam's past, present, and future.

> ### ► Building Background
> Have students look carefully through the illustrations of the book. Explain that this story is an informational narrative. It gives facts by telling a story. Tell students that one purpose for reading is to be informed. Have students set a purpose for reading *Stone Wall Secrets* by writing one or more questions they think will be answered by the book.

Vocabulary

Have pairs use the vocabulary words to make a word chain. Tell them to write the word *reluctant* vertically. Have them use letters in *reluctant* to write new words, which they can then use to build even more words. After students make their word chains, challenge them to change them into crossword puzzles and write clues for the words. See pages 158–161 for additional vocabulary activities.

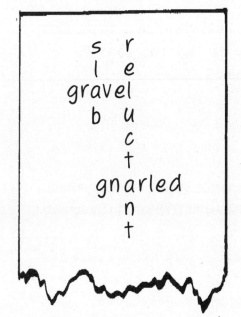

Day 1	Day 2	Day 3	Day 4
reluctant p. 3	slab p. 10	ancestors p. 23	meteorite p. 28
abruptly p. 4	gravel p. 12	artifacts p. 23	stout p. 32
quizzically p. 4	cement p. 12	relic p. 24	
gnarled p. 7	glacier p. 14		
kaleidoscope p. 9			

	Response	Strategies	Skills
Day 1 Pages 1–9	**Book Talk** • Characters' Emotions • Synthesize • Draw Conclusions **Writing:** Personal Response	**USE DECODING/ PHONICS** `FOCUS STRATEGY`	**GRAPHIC AIDS** `FOCUS SKILL` *Distant Voyages* pp. T294–T295
Day 2 Pages 10–19	**Book Talk** • Main Idea • Author's Craft • Draw Conclusions **Writing:** Characters' Emotions	Summarize	Prefixes, Suffixes, and Roots *Distant Voyages* pp. T44–T45
Day 3 Pages 20–27	**Book Talk** • Summarize • Characters' Traits • Author's Viewpoint **Writing:** Express Personal Opinions	Self-Question	Narrative Elements *Distant Voyages* pp. T68–T69
Day 4 Pages 28–37	**Book Talk** • Make Comparisons • Main Idea • Express Personal Opinions **Writing:** Personal Response	**USE DECODING/ PHONICS** `FOCUS STRATEGY`	**GRAPHIC AIDS** `FOCUS SKILL` *Distant Voyages* pp. T294–T295

Day 5
Wrap-Up

Project
✓ Make a Rock Display
• Inquiry Project

Writing
✓ Paragraph of Information

Language Link
• Adjectives

Assessment
✓ Comprehension Test

*Additional support is provided in *Trophies*.
✓ Options for Assessment

© Harcourt

Stone Wall Secrets

BOOK TALK

After you read pages 1–9, meet with your group to discuss and answer the following questions:

1 How does the grandfather feel about selling stones from the wall?

2 How does the grandfather teach Adam about the rocks around the homestead?

3 What does the sand inside the rock reveal about the land?

RESPONSE JOURNAL

Does anyone you know collect rocks or treasure something made of stones? If so, tell why.

Strategies Good Readers Use

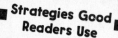

FOCUS STRATEGY USE DECODING/ PHONICS

Review pages 1–9 and make a list of words you might have difficulty reading aloud. Split each word into syllables and practice saying the words aloud until you feel more comfortable with them.

SKILLS IN CONTEXT

FOCUS SKILL **GRAPHIC AIDS: USING ILLUSTRATIONS TO UNDERSTAND A STORY** The illustrations in a story often help you understand certain events. Revisit pages 1–9 of *Stone Wall Secrets* and tell how the illustrations help clarify the story.

What You Need

- paper
- pen or pencil

What to Do

1. Skim pages 1–9 for illustrations.

2. Guess what event each illustration is portraying.

3. On a piece of notebook paper, list which page each illustration appears on. Next to each page number, write one or two sentences telling which story event the illustration is describing.

4. Share your list with a classmate.

Here is an example to get you started:
Page 1 shows the old man standing on the porch of his farmhouse, staring at the old stone wall.

Think Ahead
What else will Adam's grandfather show him?

© Harcourt

Stone Wall Secrets

BOOK TALK

After you read pages 10–19, meet with your group to discuss and answer the following questions:

1. How can a rock be from both the ocean and a mountain?

2. Why do the authors use the grandfather to tell about stones and rocks and how they are formed?

3. How do you know that Adam is interested in his grandfather's stories about rocks?

RESPONSE JOURNAL

What is Adam thinking and feeling as his grandfather tells him about the past? What would you be thinking and feeling?

Strategies Good Readers Use

SUMMARIZE

Remember that when you summarize a passage, you briefly retell the most important events or ideas. Choose a passage from pages 10–19 and summarize it.

SKILLS IN CONTEXT

PREFIXES, SUFFIXES, AND ROOTS: PLAY A SUFFIX GAME There are many words with suffixes in *Stone Wall Secrets*. *Abruptly* is made from the word *abrupt* plus the suffix *-ly*. The suffix *-ly* means "in this way." It turns an adjective, such as *abrupt*, into an adverb. *Grainy* is made from the word *grain* plus the suffix *-y*. The suffix *-y* means "having." It turns a noun, such as *grain*, into an adjective. When you add a suffix to a word, you slightly change the word's meaning. Play a suffix game with a partner.

What You Need

- seventeen index cards
- writing materials

What to Do

1. Write one of these words on each of the cards: *rock, rain, milk, deep, mud, slab, ice, gust, real, eventual, sponge, quick, final, shade, safe, strange, wind.*

2. Mix up the cards. Take turns with your partner and draw a card.

3. Write a new word that ends with *-y* or *-ly* for each word you draw. You can use pages 10–19 of your book to help you. Each new word appears there. Note that the spelling of some words may change once you add a suffix.

4. Use the new word in a sentence about Adam, his grandfather, or the stones.

Here is a sentence to get you started: *The earth feels* spongy *right after the snow melts.*

Think Ahead
What other parts of the history of the farm will Grampa tell about?

© Harcourt

Stone Wall Secrets

BOOK TALK

After you read pages 20–27, meet with your group to discuss and answer the following questions:

1 What do you learn on pages 20–27 about how Grampa's land has changed?

2 What does the trick that Grampa plays on Adam reveal about Grampa?

3 How do you think the authors of this book feel about stone walls and old rocks?

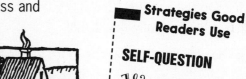

Strategies Good Readers Use

SELF-QUESTION

*W*rite down one question that you asked yourself as you read this part of the book. Also write down the answer.

RESPONSE JOURNAL

What do you think you would enjoy about visiting Adam's grandfather's farm?

SKILLS IN CONTEXT

NARRATIVE ELEMENTS: MAKE A POSTER This book is full of facts, but it uses narrative elements to tell those facts. The characters are the people in the book. The setting is the time and place in which the story takes place. The plot is the set of events that makes up the story. The narrative elements help you understand the facts in this story. Work in a small group to create a poster that shows the characters, the setting, and the plot of this story.

What You Need

- **paper or poster board**
- **writing and drawing materials**

What to Do

1. Identify the characters, the setting, and the plot, so far, of the story. Be sure to identify the problem as well.

2. Plan a poster to show these elements. Make the poster attractive by drawing a stone wall border or by adding other illustrations.

3. Give your poster a title. Copy your final ideas onto the poster board or paper. Use color, large letters, borders, and other methods of adding visual interest.

4. Hang your poster in the classroom.

To help you get started, here are the characters: Adam and his grandfather

Think Ahead What decision will Adam and his grandfather make about selling the stones?

© Harcourt

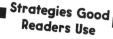

BOOK TALK

After you read pages 28–37, meet with your group to discuss and answer the following questions:

❶ *Stone Wall Secrets* is about our Earth and how it changes. What selections in *Distant Voyages* are also about change over time?

❷ What do you think the authors want readers to learn from this book?

❸ What did you like best about this book?

RESPONSE JOURNAL

What items from your own family's past do you wish that you had?

Strategies Good Readers Use

FOCUS STRATEGY USE DECODING/ PHONICS

Skim pages 28–37 for words with familiar patterns, such as words with the VCCV letter pattern. Then find other words with other familiar letter patterns, write the words on paper, and group them into their own special categories. Be sure to label each category with the letter pattern under which each word appears.

SKILLS IN CONTEXT

FOCUS SKILL **GRAPHIC AIDS: MAKE AN ILLUSTRATION** Pictures and illustrations are often helpful when trying to understand a story event. There are many illustrations in *Stone Wall Secrets*. Each illustration helps to describe an event in the story. Create your own illustration that describes an event in the story that is not illustrated.

What You Need

- **markers or colored pencils**
- **construction paper**

What to Do

1. Reread pages 28–37 to find a story event.

2. On a piece of construction paper, illustrate the story event.

3. Show your illustration to a classmate and have him or her guess which story event you chose to portray.

Here is a story event to get you started: *Adam reads the letter Grandpa wrote him.*

© Harcourt

Wrap-Up

▶ **Project** **MAKE A ROCK DISPLAY** Adam learns a great deal about rocks in this story. What did the students learn? Explain that their job is to create a rock display.

- Organize students into small groups.
- Ask groups to begin planning by completing the copying master on page 77.
- Provide time for students to look at and discuss one another's rock displays.

▶ **Writing** **PARAGRAPH OF INFORMATION** Have students respond to the following writing prompt: **Write a paragraph of information about rocks.** Have students use the copying master on page 78 to plan their paragraph. Remind them to focus on sentence fluency. Rubrics for evaluating student writing are provided on pages 154–157.

▶ **Language Link** **ADJECTIVES** Remind students that adjectives are words that modify nouns or pronouns. Have students list ten or more of the adjectives they find in this story. Ask them to also write the noun each adjective describes.

Inquiry Project

Stone Wall Secrets can be a springboard for inquiry into a variety of topics, such as meteorites, campfire stones, and glacial remains. Have students choose a topic and take notes on their research. Students can use reference books and the Internet to begin their inquiry project.

> Meteorites
> —have been found on every continent
> —generally weigh only one pound, but some are huge
> —can create huge craters on Earth

✔ **Comprehension Test** Test students' comprehension of *Stone Wall Secrets* by having them complete the copying master on page 79.

© Harcourt

Name _____

Project Planner

In *Stone Wall Secrets*, every rock tells a story. In this project, you will display rocks and tell about them. To do so, you will examine and classify each rock and then explain what it is or shows.

☐ **Step 1.** Collect six or more small rocks with your group. If a rock is too big to move or if it is part of someone's property, draw it instead. Number your rocks 1–6.

What You Need
- index cards for labels
- writing and drawing materials
- reference sources (optional)

☐ **Step 2.** Examine the rocks by looking at them and feeling them. Think about size and color. Think about whether they are rough or smooth, shiny or dull, and rounded or jagged. Use the organizer below to record information about each rock.

Rock	Characteristics
1	
2	
3	
4	
5	
6	

☐ **Step 3.** Group the rocks. Do you think wind or water has worn down some rocks? Do you think some have been broken from other pieces? Do you think any of your rocks might be cement? If you wish, use reference sources to learn about the rock.

☐ **Step 4.** Make a display. Group similar rocks together. For each rock, make a card. Present as much information as you can about each rock.

☐ **Step 5.** Put your rock display on exhibit in the classroom.

Name _____

Paragraph of Information

Write a paragraph of information about rocks. Select one main idea that you learned by reading this book. Write it at the beginning of your paragraph. Then complete your paragraph with details that support the main idea. Use the graphic organizer below to help you plan your paragraph.

Prewriting Graphic Organizer

Main Idea: _____

Detail 1: _____

_____

_____

Detail 2: _____

_____

_____

Detail 3: _____

_____

_____

Concluding Sentence: _____

_____

© Harcourt

Name _____

Comprehension Test

Read each question below. Then mark the letter for the answer you have chosen.

1. **Why does Adam's grandfather take him on a tour of his land?**
   - Ⓐ He is about to sell the land.
   - Ⓑ He is giving Adam the land.
   - Ⓒ Someone wants to buy the land.
   - Ⓓ Someone wants to buy the stones on the land.

2. **When does the action with Adam and his grandfather take place?**
   - Ⓕ in the present in the spring
   - Ⓖ in the present in the fall
   - Ⓗ in the recent past
   - Ⓙ in the distant past

3. **What time period is the grainy stone from?**
   - Ⓐ the time of the first people
   - Ⓑ the time of the first settlers who farmed and cleared the land
   - Ⓒ the time when an ocean covered the land
   - Ⓓ the time when a meteorite struck the earth

4. **Which is the correct order?**
   - Ⓕ woodland animals, tundra, glacier
   - Ⓖ glacier, woodland animals, tundra
   - Ⓗ tundra, glacier, woodland animals
   - Ⓙ glacier, tundra, woodland animals

5. **Who were the first people on Adam's grandfather's land?**
   - Ⓐ the original Americans
   - Ⓑ woodland Indians
   - Ⓒ the Pilgrims
   - Ⓓ settlers from Europe

6. **What is one reason Adam's grandfather values the stone walls so much?**
   - Ⓕ He built most of them.
   - Ⓖ He built two and helped build others.
   - Ⓗ He helped build them all.
   - Ⓙ His father and grandfathers built them all.

7. **How did the meteorite get to Adam's grandfather's farm?**
   - Ⓐ It was carried there by the glacier.
   - Ⓑ It fell from the sky.
   - Ⓒ It came from a museum.
   - Ⓓ It was brought by a stonemason.

8. **What was the main reason stone walls were built?**
   - Ⓕ The stones were in the farmers' way and had to go somewhere.
   - Ⓖ The stones made beautiful walls.
   - Ⓗ The stones were used to show boundaries.
   - Ⓙ The stones were the only materials available for fences.

9. **What do the authors mean when they say the stones on Adam's grandfather's farm are "like a library"?**
   - Ⓐ The stones can be borrowed and returned.
   - Ⓑ The stones have been gathered into one place.
   - Ⓒ The stones tell information about the past.
   - Ⓓ The stones are made like books.

10. **On a separate sheet of paper, write a short answer in response to the question below.**
    Will the stones be sold? How do you know?

The Young Artist

Reading Level

by Thomas Locker

Theme Connection

The main character of *The Young Artist* struggles with whether and how to speak the truth in his creative art. Each character is helped by a relationship with a supportive teacher.

Summary

Adrian, a twelve-year-old artist, is apprenticed to a master artist, who teaches him to paint subjects realistically and truthfully. The young artist then faces a difficult challenge when he is commanded to paint a group portrait of royal courtiers who want him to paint them without their personal flaws.

Building Background

Ask students if it is always good to tell the truth. Ask volunteers to tell about situations in which someone was hurt by hearing the truth. Tell students that in *The Young Artist*, the main character wants to show only the truth in his painting. Have students read to find out if this becomes a problem. Tell students that *The Young Artist* is historical fiction that appears to take place in the Netherlands. Have students locate the Netherlands on a globe, and ask what images the country brings to mind. Tell students to note details in the illustrations as they read to verify the setting.

Author Profile

Thomas Locker has attained a national reputation as a talented landscape artist, and he has also written and illustrated several award-winning children's books. *Publisher's Weekly* noted that Locker's illustrations "elegantly recall old Dutch masters."

Additional Books by the Author
• *Where the River Begins*
• *The Boy Who Held Back the Sea*
• *Sailing with the Wind*

Vocabulary

Have students work in pairs to create sentences using vocabulary words. Ask volunteers to write sentences on the board, leaving a blank in place of each vocabulary word. Have other students use context to determine the correct words to complete sentences. See pages 158–161 for additional vocabulary activities.

Paul wanted to swim, but he agreed _____ to mow the lawn.

Day 1	Day 2	Day 3	Day 4
portrait p. 2	vowed p. 10	humble p. 16	inspired p. 22
reluctantly p. 2	rework p. 12	contemptuously p. 16	outraged p. 26
apprentice p. 4	masterpiece p. 12	dismay p. 16	
criticized p. 8	compromise p. 14	courtiers p. 18	

© Harcourt

	Response	Strategies	Skills
▶ Day 1 **Pages 1–9**	**Book Talk** • Draw Conclusions • Characters' Traits • Characters' Emotions **Writing:** Write a Letter	**MAKE AND CONFIRM PREDICTIONS** `FOCUS STRATEGY`	**WORD RELATIONSHIPS** `FOCUS SKILL` *Distant Voyages* pp. T388–T389
▶ Day 2 **Pages 10–15**	**Book Talk** • Characters' Motivations • Cause-Effect • Characters' Emotions **Writing:** Draw Conclusions	Self-Question	Narrative Elements *Distant Voyages* pp. T68–T69
▶ Day 3 **Pages 16–21**	**Book Talk** • Draw Conclusions • Summarize • Characters' Emotions **Writing:** Write Advice for a Character	Read Ahead	Text Structure: Sequence *Distant Voyages* pp. T295A–T295B
▶ Day 4 **Pages 22–29**	**Book Talk** • Make Comparisons • Theme • Make Judgments **Writing:** Express Personal Opinions	**MAKE AND CONFIRM PREDICTIONS** `FOCUS STRATEGY`	**WORD RELATIONSHIPS** `FOCUS SKILL` *Distant Voyages* pp. T388–T389
▶ Day 5 **Wrap-Up**	**Project** ✓ Create an Art Show Catalog • Inquiry Project **Writing** ✓ Persuasive Letter **Language Link** • Vivid Verbs **Assessment** ✓ Comprehension Test		

*Additional support is provided in *Trophies*.
✓ Options for Assessment

The Young Artist

BOOK TALK

After you read pages 1–9, meet with your group to discuss and answer the following questions:

1 The narrator had stopped teaching years ago, but he agrees to teach Adrian. Why?

2 How is Adrian different from other apprentices the narrator has taught in the past?

3 Although Adrian is a talented artist, the narrator worries about his future. Why?

RESPONSE JOURNAL

Adrian leaves home and comes to live with a master artist to learn the artist's craft. Imagine that you are Adrian, and write a letter to your parents, telling about your experiences as an artist's apprentice.

SKILLS IN CONTEXT

FOCUS SKILL **WORD RELATIONSHIPS: SYNONYM GAME** When two words are synonyms, they have the same or almost the same meaning. Revisit *The Young Artist* to find synonyms for words that you are having difficulty understanding.

What You Need

- pen or pencil
- paper
- thesaurus
- dictionary

What to Do

1. Review pages 1–9 of the book. Choose ten words from the story that you do not understand.

2. Use a thesaurus to find synonyms for the ten words.

3. On a piece of paper, write the words you do not understand and what you think they might mean, based on your understanding of each word's synonym.

4. Then look up each word in a dictionary and find out if your definition is correct. You should have a better understanding of the words.

Here are some words to get you started: strokes, reluctantly, apprentices

Think Ahead

Why do you think the narrator "made a terrible mistake" when he asked Adrian to paint the chef's portrait?

© Harcourt

The Young Artist

BOOK TALK

After you read pages 10–15, meet with your group to discuss and answer the following questions:

1 Why does Adrian refuse to change the chef's portrait?

2 What prompts Adrian to vow never to paint another portrait?

3 How and why do Adrian's feelings change as he travels to the castle?

RESPONSE JOURNAL

The king is feared throughout the land, and no one wants a picture of his castle. What, if anything, do you think Adrian has to fear from the king? Explain.

Strategies Good Readers Use

SELF-QUESTION

Good readers ask themselves questions as they read. Write one question that you asked yourself while reading, and tell how using this strategy helped you understand the story.

SKILLS IN CONTEXT

NARRATIVE ELEMENTS: PLOT, CHARACTER, AND SETTING PYRAMID The basic ingredients of a story are plot (what happens in the story), character (who the story is about), and setting (where and when the story takes place). Make a three-sided display that highlights the narrative elements of plot, character, and setting in *The Young Artist*.

What You Need

- square sheet of construction paper (12 inch square)
- pencils and markers

What to Do

1. Divide the construction paper into four triangles by folding it in half diagonally in both directions. Unfold.
2. Cut away and discard one triangle. Label the three remaining triangles *Plot*, *Character*, and *Setting*.
3. Under *Plot*, list major story events in order.
4. Under *Character*, list the main characters and some adjectives that describe each one.
5. Under *Setting*, write where and when the story takes place.
6. Bring together the cut edges so your writing faces out, and tape into a three-sided pyramid.
7. Share your pyramid with classmates.

Here is an adjective that describes Adrian to get you started: idealistic

Think Ahead Why do you think Adrian has been summoned to the castle?

© Harcourt

The Young Artist

BOOK TALK

After you read pages 16–21, meet with your group to discuss and answer the following questions:

1 Why does Adrian's project seem like a nightmare?

2 Why does the narrator blame himself for Adrian's problem, and what does he do about it?

3 What does Adrian mean when he says, "To paint twenty-six lies is no honor"?

> ### Strategies Good Readers Use
>
> **READ AHEAD**
>
> How do you think Adrian will handle his problem? Read ahead a few pages to find out whether your prediction was correct.

RESPONSE JOURNAL

Adrian is about to begin "the most difficult time of his life." What advice would you give him?

SKILLS IN CONTEXT

TEXT STRUCTURE: SEQUENCE: STORY MAP   In *The Young Artist* the narrator tells events in the order in which they happen, or sequence. Time-order words like *first*, *next*, and *finally* help you follow the sequence of events. Make a sequence story map that records the events in the order in which they happen.

What You Need

- **construction paper**
- **scissors, markers**
- **pencil**

What to Do

1. Cut construction paper into arrow-shaped strips. When writing on the strips, be sure all arrows point to the right.

2. Write *Adrian's father visits the narrator's studio.* on the first strip.

3. Write *Adrian is given a room in the castle tower.* on the last strip.

4. On the other strips, write the story events that happen between these two occurrences.

5. Arrange the strips into the correct story sequence. Refer to the book if necessary.

6. Display the strips in the proper order on a classroom wall.

Here is an event to include in the middle of the sequence: *The chef sees his portrait a second time and likes it.*

Adrian's father visits the narrator's studio.

Think Ahead What do you think Adrian will do at the castle?

The Young Artist

BOOK TALK

After you read pages 22–29, meet with your group to discuss and answer the following questions:

1 Adrian refuses to compromise and change his painting of the chef. What other characters from *Distant Voyages* make similarly courageous choices? Explain.

2 What are some important themes in *The Young Artist*?

3 Do you believe Adrian should have given in to the courtiers' demands? Why or why not?

Strategies Good Readers Use

FOCUS STRATEGY **MAKE AND CONFIRM PREDICTIONS**

*R*ecall two or three predictions you made as you read *The Young Artist*. Did you revise any of them as your reading progressed?

RESPONSE JOURNAL

What is your opinion of the king? Does he treat nobles fairly? Is he fair to Adrian?

SKILLS IN CONTEXT

 WORD RELATIONSHIPS: MULTIPLE-MEANING WORDS Some words have more than one meaning. For example, the word *brush* can mean *a tool having hairs, fastened to a back or handle, used for grooming.* It can also mean *a growth of small trees and shrubs.* Find words in *The Young Artist* that have multiple-meanings.

What You Need

- **dictionary**
- **pen or pencil**
- **paper**

What to Do

1. Revisit pages 22–29 of *The Young Artist*. Search for words that have multiple-meanings.

2. On a piece of paper, list the words. Next to the words, make two columns.

3. In the first column, write the definitions of the words in the context of the story.

4. Use a dictionary to find meanings for the words that are different from the meanings of the words as they are used in the story.

5. Record these meanings in the second column. When you are finished, share your words and their multiple-meanings with a classmate.

Here are some words to get you started:
tower, light, well, band

Wrap-Up

▶ **Project** **CREATE AN ART SHOW CATALOG** Tell students that when artists, such as Thomas Locker, exhibit their work, viewers are given a show catalog to help them appreciate and learn about the artwork. Tell students they will create a catalog for Adrian's first exhibit.

- Organize students in groups to discuss how such a catalog can help viewers.
- Ask students to complete the copying master on page 87 to plan their catalogs.
- Have students create their catalogs. Students may wish to use a word processing program to publish their catalogs.
- Have each group present its finished catalog to the class.

▶ **Writing** **PERSUASIVE LETTER** Have students respond to the following writing prompt: **Write a persuasive letter that Adrian might write to his teacher, explaining why he cannot paint the courtiers differently than he sees them.** Have students use the copying master on page 88 to plan their letters. Remind students to focus on word choice. Rubrics for evaluating student writing are provided on pages 154–157.

▶ **Language Link** **VIVID VERBS** Explain to students that the author uses many vivid verbs to indicate how a character is speaking. For example, characters in the book "hissed" and "shrieked." Have students find other examples of vivid verbs from this and other books and ask them to make a list of the verbs.

Inquiry Project

The Young Artist can stimulate students' interest in a variety of topics. Have students brainstorm topics they would like to know more about and organize their responses into a web. After choosing a topic, students may use reference books and the Internet to begin their inquiry projects.

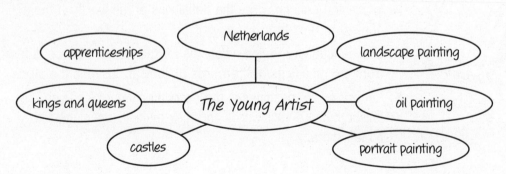

✔ **Comprehension Test** Test students' comprehension of *The Young Artist* by having them complete the copying master on page 89.

Name _____

Project Planner

Imagine that Adrian's first exhibit as a professional artist is opening soon, and you are going to create a catalog for the show. Art show catalogs usually give a brief biography of the artist and provide the titles and descriptions of each piece of artwork on display.

☐ **Step 1.** List details about Adrian's life to include in a short biography.

_____

_____

_____

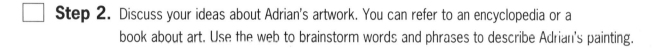

What You Need
- paper
- pencils and markers OR computer and printer
- reference sources

☐ **Step 2.** Discuss your ideas about Adrian's artwork. You can refer to an encyclopedia or a book about art. Use the web to brainstorm words and phrases to describe Adrian's painting.

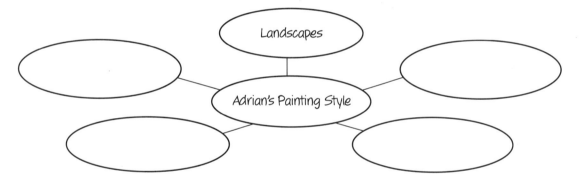

Landscapes

Adrian's Painting Style

☐ **Step 3.** Use the information from your web to help you write titles and descriptions of at least three paintings Adrian would be likely to create. Use the lines on the paintings below.

  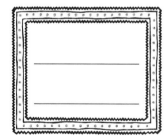

☐ **Step 4.** Work together to create your art show catalog, using either folded paper and markers or a computer and a word processing program.

☐ **Step 5.** As a group, present your catalog to the class.

© Harcourt

Persuasive Letter

Write a persuasive letter that Adrian might write to his teacher, explaining why he cannot paint the courtiers differently than he sees them. Use your knowledge about Adrian's character and actions to figure out how he might think. Use the graphic organizer below to plan your letter.

Prewriting Graphic Organizer

Topic: _____

Audience: _____

Opinion: _____

Reason 1: _____

Details: _____

Reason 2: _____

Details: _____

Reason 3: _____

Details: _____

Conclusion: _____

_____

© Harcourt

Name _____

Comprehension Test

Read each question below. Then mark the letter for the answer you have chosen.

1. **What does Adrian most want to learn?**

   Ⓐ how to paint portraits

   Ⓑ how to sketch the princess

   Ⓒ how to paint landscapes

   Ⓓ how to paint while people are watching

2. **Which is *not* one of the reasons the narrator encourages Adrian to paint portraits?**

   Ⓕ A good portrait painter is always in demand.

   Ⓖ Adrian is good at painting pictures of people.

   Ⓗ Adrian will not have to worry about earning a living if he paints portraits.

   Ⓙ The narrator vows never to paint again.

3. **As an apprentice, Adrian spends his free time**

   Ⓐ sketching in the countryside.

   Ⓑ trying to gain entry into the castle.

   Ⓒ sweeping the studio.

   Ⓓ perfecting his skill as a portrait artist.

4. **Why does Adrian speak "furiously" to his teacher when they discuss the chef's portrait?**

   Ⓕ The teacher says he can do a better job.

   Ⓖ Adrian feels his teacher wants him to paint a lie.

   Ⓗ The teacher keeps the chef's payment.

   Ⓙ Adrian thinks that he is a better portrait painter than his teacher is.

5. **Which word does *not* describe Adrian?**

   Ⓐ practical   Ⓒ idealistic

   Ⓑ talented   Ⓓ stubborn

6. **Why does Adrian find it easier to paint the princess than the courtiers?**

   Ⓕ She does not ask him to paint her differently than he sees her.

   Ⓖ It is easier because she is a child.

   Ⓗ He can draw her from memory.

   Ⓙ He practiced sketching her as an apprentice.

7. **When Adrian returns after seeking advice about the group portrait, the narrator thinks he will never see Adrian again. Why?**

   Ⓐ He fears that Adrian is angry with him.

   Ⓑ He thinks that it will take Adrian forever to paint twenty-six portraits.

   Ⓒ Adrian will enjoy living in the castle.

   Ⓓ He fears the King's anger if Adrian disobeys the king's order.

8. **Why does the princess warn the king?**

   Ⓕ Adrian is not working on the painting.

   Ⓖ The nobles bully and badger Adrian.

   Ⓗ Courtiers are on the way to disturb Adrian.

   Ⓙ Adrian's work is false and lifeless.

9. **Why does Adrian finish the group portrait "in no time at all" after the king visits?**

   Ⓐ He already has a good start on it.

   Ⓑ He no longer has to paint a lie.

   Ⓒ He has been able to get more paints.

   Ⓓ He knows the king will reward him.

10. **On a separate sheet of paper, write a short answer in response to this question:** When Adrian's apprentice is ready to start his own career, what advice might Adrian give him?

© Harcourt

Dear Benjamin Banneker

Reading Level

by Andrea Davis Pinkney

Theme Connection

As students read *Dear Benjamin Banneker*, they will learn about another important American. Banneker made significant contributions to his country through his determination and creative endeavors.

Summary

Born a free man in 1731, Benjamin Banneker became an accomplished astronomer, mathematician, and almanac author. Banneker also became an early hero in the struggle for emancipation by setting an example of excellence and by speaking out against slavery to one of the leading statesmen of his time, Thomas Jefferson.

Building Background

Explain that *Dear Benjamin Banneker* is an informational narrative that tells about the life of an African American man who lived during colonial times. Have students name important Americans who lived during the colonial period. Have them read to find out why Benjamin Banneker is an important American.

Author Profile

Andrea Davis Pinkney has written several critically acclaimed children's books. Many have been illustrated by her husband, Brian Pinkney, who won a Caldecott Honor award in 1999 for *Duke Ellington: The Piano Prince and His Orchestra*. Andrea Davis Pinkney has also written for such publications as *The New York Times* and *Highlights for Children*.

Additional Books by the Author

- *Bill Pickett: Rodeo Ridin' Cowboy*
- *Alvin Ailey*

Vocabulary

Have students sort the vocabulary words into categories such as the following: scientific terms; words with prefixes and suffixes; describing words. See pages 158–161 for additional vocabulary activities.

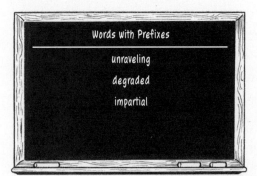

Words with Prefixes

unraveling

degraded

impartial

Day 1	Day 2	Day 3	Day 4
hypocrite p. 2	calculate p. 8	abolition p. 17	degraded p. 25
almanac p. 3	eclipses p. 10	distinguished p. 21	ardently p. 25
grueling p. 6	unraveling p. 12	tyranny p. 23	commenced p. 25
cycles p. 6		benevolence p. 23	
		impartial p. 23	

	Response	Strategies	Skills
▶ Day 1 **Pages 2–7**	**Book Talk** • Author's Purpose • Compare and Contrast • Characters' Traits **Writing:** Evaluate Author's Note	**READ AHEAD** FOCUS STRATEGY	**FACT AND OPINION** FOCUS SKILL *Distant Voyages* pp. T420–T421
▶ Day 2 **Pages 8–15**	**Book Talk** • Characters' Traits • Draw Conclusions • Speculate **Writing:** Personal Response	Use Context to Confirm Meaning	Make Judgments *Distant Voyages* pp. T112–T113
▶ Day 3 **Pages 16–23**	**Book Talk** • Important Details • Important Details • Draw Conclusions **Writing:** Express Personal Opinions	Adjust Reading Rate	Narrative Elements *Distant Voyages* pp. T68–T69
▶ Day 4 **Pages 24–30**	**Book Talk** • Compare and Contrast • Theme • Speculate **Writing:** Write from the Perspective of a Character	**READ AHEAD** FOCUS STRATEGY	**FACT AND OPINION** FOCUS SKILL *Distant Voyages* pp. T420–T421
▶ Day 5 **Wrap-Up**	**Project** ✓ Create a Knowledge Game • Inquiry Project **Writing** ✓ Research Report **Language Link** • Similes **Assessment** ✓ Comprehension Test		

*Additional support is provided in *Trophies*.
✓ Options for Assessment

© Harcourt

Dear Benjamin Banneker

BOOK TALK

After you read pages 2–7, meet with your group to discuss and answer the following questions:

1 What do you think is Andrea Davis Pinkney's purpose for writing the Author's Note?

2 How did being a free man set Benjamin Banneker apart from most African Americans of his time?

3 What character traits did Banneker have as a child that might have helped him become a scientist?

RESPONSE JOURNAL

Do you find the Author's Note interesting or helpful? In a journal entry, explain your feelings about reading that section of the book.

Strategies Good Readers Use

FOCUS STRATEGY **READ AHEAD**

Think about a time when you read ahead to figure something out. How did using this strategy help you better understand what you were reading?

SKILLS IN CONTEXT

FOCUS SKILL **FACT AND OPINION: FACT/OPINION FLIP** Facts are ideas that can be proven. Opinions are ideas that are personal beliefs. Play a game in which you flip things around. Turn facts into opinions and opinions into facts.

What You Need

- pencils
- small index cards

What to Do

1. Look through pages 2–7 of *Dear Benjamin Banneker* to look for examples of facts and opinions. Write each on a separate index card.

2. Arrange the cards face down on a table or desk. Take turns choosing one card. Read the card aloud and identify it as either fact or opinion. Then flip the idea. If you picked a fact, turn it into a related opinion. If you picked an opinion, turn it into a related fact.

3. Keep the card if you successfully flip the idea. If you do not flip the idea, put the card back for someone else to try.

Here are a fact and an opinion to get you started: Fact: *Benjamin Banneker created an almanac.* Opinion: *He was an accomplished scientist.*

Think Ahead
How does Banneker learn about the stars and moon?

© Harcourt

Dear Benjamin Banneker

BOOK TALK

After you read pages 8–15, meet with your group to discuss and answer the following questions:

1 Benjamin Banneker taught himself astronomy at night, after he had worked all day. What does this tell you about him?

2 Almanacs are still published, but they are not considered as valuable today as they were long ago. Why might this be true?

3 Why do you think several publishers refused to publish Banneker's almanac?

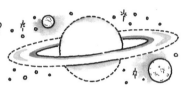

RESPONSE JOURNAL

Benjamin Banneker began to lose faith in his almanac when he couldn't find a publisher. Write a journal entry about a time when something happened that made you question your own abilities.

Strategies Good Readers Use

USE CONTEXT TO CONFIRM MEANING

The meaning of a word often depends on how it is used in a story. List some of the words whose meanings you checked by thinking about the words and sentences around them.

SKILLS IN CONTEXT

MAKE JUDGMENTS: JUDGMENT CHART When you read a biography, you sometimes make judgments about whether a person is right or wrong, based on his or her actions. Your judgment is valid if there is enough evidence to support it. Make judgments about Benjamin Banneker, based on what you learn about him through events and details in the book.

What You Need

- notebook paper
- writing materials

What to Do

1. Divide a piece of notebook paper into two columns. Label the left column *Judgment* and label the right column *Evidence*.

2. Make a judgment about Benjamin Banneker, based on what you have learned about him so far. Write your judgment in the column of your notebook paper labeled *Judgment*.

3. Reread pages 8–15. Find evidence from the text that supports your judgment. In the column labeled *Evidence*, record the evidence.

4. Continue this procedure two or three times until your chart is full. Share your findings with the class.

Here's an idea to get you started:
Benjamin worked long hours to make sure his farm would yield healthy crops.

Think Ahead
Do you think Benjamin Banneker will find a publisher?

Dear Benjamin Banneker

BOOK TALK

After you read pages 16–23, meet with your group to discuss and answer the following questions:

1 Why did Benjamin Banneker worry that most black people would not be able to use his almanac?

2 What was Banneker's main reason for writing a letter to Thomas Jefferson?

3 Why do you think Banneker sent a copy of his almanac with the letter?

RESPONSE JOURNAL

Imagine that you live in Benjamin Banneker's time. Write a journal entry that describes your feelings about slavery.

Strategies Good Readers Use

ADJUST READING RATE

Good readers adjust their pace of reading depending on the difficulty of the material. Write about a time when your reading rate slowed because the text was hard to read. How did this strategy help you read that section?

SKILLS IN CONTEXT

NARRATIVE ELEMENTS: BIOGRAPHICAL COMIC STRIP Plot, setting, and character are the elements of a narrative. Plot is the sequence of events. Setting is where and when the story takes place. Characters are the people in the story. A comic strip shares the elements of a narrative. It tells a story using pictures and speech bubbles.

What You Need

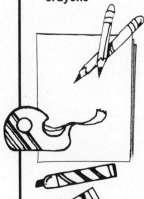

- **unlined paper**
- **tape or stapler**
- **pencils**
- **markers or crayons**

What to Do

1. Form a small group. Decide what event in Banneker's life your group will show in your comic strip.

2. Draw a series of squares. In each square, make notes about the characters, events, and setting you want to show.

3. Have each member of the group draw and color a separate panel of the comic strip. Put the characters' words in speech bubbles.

4. Tape or staple your panels together in order to make a strip.

Here is an idea to get you started: *For a comic strip about the publication of Banneker's almanac, the first panel could show a meeting of several abolitionists. One could be saying to another, "This man's almanac should be published!"*

Think Ahead
How do you think Jefferson will respond to Banneker's letter?

© Harcourt

Dear Benjamin Banneker

BOOK TALK

Meet with your group to discuss and answer the following questions:

1 What stories in *Distant Voyages* remind you of situations or events described in *Dear Benjamin Banneker?*

2 What is the theme of this book?

3 If Benjamin Banneker lived now, what contributions do you think he might make to the world?

Strategies Good Readers Use

FOCUS STRATEGY **READ AHEAD**

*R*eading ahead is one way to check the meaning of a word. List some words for which you used this strategy.

RESPONSE JOURNAL

Imagine that Benjamin Banneker could time-travel to the 21st century. Write a journal entry that he might write about the progress of civil rights in America.

SKILLS IN CONTEXT

FOCUS SKILL **FACT AND OPINION: FACTS AND OPINIONS ABOUT BENJAMIN BANNEKER** Facts are ideas that can be proven. Opinions are ideas that are personal beliefs; they can differ from person to person. Make a book in which you show facts and opinions about Benjamin Banneker.

What You Need

- paper
- writing and drawing tools
- construction paper
- stapler

What to Do

1. Review facts that you learned about Benjamin Banneker as you read the book. Form your own opinion about each fact you learned.

2. On a piece of paper, list each fact. Write your opinion underneath each fact.

3. Copy each statement and fact to the bottom of each piece of construction paper. Illustrate each page.

4. On another piece of construction paper, create a cover for your book. Illustrate the cover, add a title, and add yourself as the author.

5. Share your book with a classmate. Take turns reading each other's books.

Here is a fact to get you started: *Benjamin spent close to a year observing the sky at night.*

Wrap-Up

▶ **Project** **CREATE A KNOWLEDGE GAME** Remind students that *Dear Benjamin Banneker* is a story based on facts about Banneker and his life. Explain that they are going to create board games that will help them review what they learned about this famous American.

- Arrange students into groups and have them discuss game formats.
- Ask each group to complete the copying master on page 97 to plan its game.
- Have the groups create, present, and play their games.

▶ **Writing** **RESEARCH REPORT** Ask students to respond to the following writing prompt: **What are the major accomplishments of Benjamin Banneker?** Tell students to focus on organization. Have students use the copying master on page 98 to plan their research reports. Rubrics for evaluating student writing are provided on pages 154–157.

▶ **Language Link** **SIMILES** Explain that the author uses a simile when she writes that Banneker's faith in his almanac started to "shrivel, like the logs burning in his fireplace." A simile uses the words *like* or *as* to make a comparison between two things that are not alike. Have students write a simile to describe the moon, the stars, the sky at night, or the sun.

Inquiry Project

Dear Benjamin Banneker can inspire inquiry into a number of related topics and ideas. Have students brainstorm a list of things they would like to learn more about, such as the abolitionist movement or Thomas Jefferson. Invite them to use reference books and the Internet to research their topics. Ask students to record their questions and the answers they find on note cards.

> **Who were some famous abolitionists?**
> William Lloyd Garrison, Lucretia Mott, John Brown
> from *New World Encyclopedia*, page 146.

✔ **Comprehension Test** Test students' comprehension of *Dear Benjamin Banneker* by having them complete the copying master on page 99.

Name _____

Project Planner

Use what you have learned about Benjamin Banneker to create a board game. Playing the game will test your knowledge, and it will be a fun way to review what you have learned!

☐ **Step 1.** Discuss with your group the types of questions you want to include, such as multiple choice, true/false, or fill-in-the-blank. List your ideas below.

_____

_____

_____

What You Need

- research materials (books, the Internet, CD-ROMs, etc.)
- paper and pencils
- 3" x 5" index cards
- one large index card
- colored markers
- large sheet of poster board
- game materials (markers, dice or spinner, etc.)

☐ **Step 2.** Pick three types of questions to use. On the small index cards, write at least five questions for each type of question. Number the cards from *1* to *15* and record the numbered answers on a sheet of paper.

☐ **Step 3.** Discuss how your game will be played and what the rules will be. Write your ideas for the rules on the lines below. Then write the game rules on a large index card for players to use.

_____

_____

_____

☐ **Step 4.** Work together to draw a colorful game board on the poster board. Remember to include the following: spaces that ask players to choose a question card; reward and penalty spaces; spaces marked *Start* and *Finish*

☐ **Step 5.** Try out the game before inviting others to play.

PENALTY!
Goddard refuses to publish almanac. Lose a turn.

QUESTION:
Benjamin Banneker wrote a letter to _____.

© Harcourt

Name _____

Research Report

Research and report about the major accomplishments of Benjamin Banneker. Plan your report on the graphic organizer below.

Prewriting Graphic Organizer

Topic: The major accomplishments of Benjamin Banneker

Main idea of my report: _____

_____

Notes

Accomplishment: _____

_____

Accomplishment: _____

_____

Accomplishment: _____

_____

Accomplishment: _____

_____

References: _____

_____

Name _____

Comprehension Test Test Prep

Read each question below. Then mark the letter for the answer you have chosen.

1. **Why was Benjamin Banneker born free?**

   Ⓐ His parents' owner became an abolitionist.

   Ⓑ He paid for his freedom.

   Ⓒ He was born after slavery ended.

   Ⓓ His parents were free before he was born.

2. **Why was Banneker determined to create an almanac?**

   Ⓕ He understood the movements of the stars.

   Ⓖ He wanted to prove that he could do it.

   Ⓗ An abolitionist group asked him to do it.

   Ⓙ There were no good almanacs.

3. **Why were almanacs important to colonial Americans?**

   Ⓐ Almanacs gave the names of the stars.

   Ⓑ Almanacs did not cost much.

   Ⓒ Almanacs were the only books people had.

   Ⓓ Almanacs gave information about weather and growing conditions.

4. **Why was James Pemberton interested in Banneker's almanac?**

   Ⓕ He wanted a new almanac.

   Ⓖ He thought it would make money.

   Ⓗ He lived near Banneker.

   Ⓙ He worked for the rights of black people.

5. **Why did Banneker decide to speak out about slavery?**

   Ⓐ He wanted to go to the White House.

   Ⓑ Many people would use his almanac.

   Ⓒ He realized that most slaves would never be able to use his almanac.

   Ⓓ He knew he would be praised.

6. **Why did Benjamin Banneker write a letter to Thomas Jefferson?**

   Ⓕ Jefferson was the President.

   Ⓖ Jefferson was also a farmer.

   Ⓗ He wanted to express his opinion that all men should be free.

   Ⓙ Jefferson was interested in his almanac.

7. **What did Banneker want to know about Thomas Jefferson?**

   Ⓐ why Jefferson owned slaves

   Ⓑ if Jefferson would buy his almanac

   Ⓒ if Jefferson had signed the Declaration of Independence

   Ⓓ why Jefferson wanted to be President

8. **What proof was there that Banneker's almanac was successful?**

   Ⓕ Store owners sold the almanac in 1792.

   Ⓖ Slavery was ended.

   Ⓗ Jefferson bought the almanac.

   Ⓙ The first edition sold out right away.

9. **How did publishing an almanac change Banneker's life?**

   Ⓐ He was able to quit working as a farmer.

   Ⓑ He was able to go to college.

   Ⓒ He answered his questions about stars.

   Ⓓ He became famous around the world.

10. **Respond to this question:**

    In your opinion, what was Benjamin Banneker's greatest contribution to history?

© Harcourt

Frindle

Reading Level

by Andrew Clements

▶ Theme Connection

As students read *Frindle*, they will see how a group of students learns firsthand how language affects an entire community. Reading the entire book will enable them to find out what startling events occur as a result of the oath that the students sign.

▶ Summary

Nick Allen is a curious and inventive fifth-grade student. Partly because he is clever and partly as a challenge to Mrs. Granger, his language arts teacher, he invents a new word, *frindle*, which means "pen." Although Nick's invention causes an unexpected uproar at school, at home, and in the community, creative individuality and a caring, capable teacher carry the day.

▶ Building Background

Point out that *Frindle* is a realistic fiction novel and that many of the scenes take place in a fifth-grade classroom similar to the students' classroom. Explain that the main event in the story is Nick's invention of a new word, *frindle*. Ask students to identify words that have come into the English language from various sources, such as other languages (Spanish words like *patio*, *burro*, and *ranch*) and technology (*input*, *output*, and *software*). Use the examples to lead students to understand that language is constantly growing and changing.

Author Profile

Andrew Clements is a former teacher who has written several picture books for young readers. *Frindle*, his first book for middle readers, received enthusiastic reviews and several awards. He has said that it is "about discovering the true nature of words, language, thought, community, learning. It's also about great teaching and great teachers."

Additional Books by the Author
- *Big Al*
- *Workshop*
- *Billy and the Bad Teacher*
- *The Landry News*

Vocabulary

Have students use a chart like the one below to sort the vocabulary words according to parts of speech. See pages 158–161 for additional vocabulary activities.

Nouns	Verbs	Adjectives

Day 1
troublemaker p. 1
essential p. 11
complex p. 20
concentration p. 25

Day 2
disrupted p. 40
furious p. 43
conference p. 44
vandalism p. 53

Day 3
squirmed p. 60
trademark p. 72
controversial p. 76
ruckus p. 82

Day 4
celebrity p. 87
recommend p. 97
villain p. 99
scholarships p. 103

© Harcourt

	Response	Strategies	Skills
Day 1 Chapters 1–5	**Book Talk** • Characters' Traits • Characters' Motivations • Make Judgments **Writing:** Express Personal Opinions	USE CONTEXT TO CONFIRM MEANING `FOCUS STRATEGY`	TEXT STRUCTURE: COMPARE AND CONTRAST `FOCUS SKILL` *Distant Voyages* pp. T510–T511
Day 2 Chapters 6–9	**Book Talk** • Cause-Effect • Identify with Characters • Make Predictions **Writing:** Make Judgments	Summarize	Narrative Elements *Distant Voyages* pp. T68–T69
Day 3 Chapters 10–12	**Book Talk** • Cause-Effect • Characters' Traits • Characters' Motivations **Writing:** Identify with Characters	Self-Question	Text Structure: Cause and Effect *Distant Voyages* pp. T646–T647
Day 4 Chapters 13–15	**Book Talk** • Theme • Main Idea • Identify with Characters **Writing:** Characters' Emotions	USE CONTEXT TO CONFIRM MEANING `FOCUS STRATEGY`	TEXT STRUCTURE: COMPARE AND CONTRAST `FOCUS SKILL` *Distant Voyages* pp. T510–T511
Day 5 Wrap-Up	**Project** ✓ Invent New Words • Inquiry Project **Writing** ✓ Research Report **Language Link** • Images **Assessment** ✓ Comprehension Test		

*Additional support is provided in *Trophies.*
✓ Options for Assessment

Frindle

BOOK TALK

After you read Chapters 1–5, meet with your group to discuss and answer the following questions:

1 What words would you use to describe Nick Allen and Mrs. Granger?

2 Why might Mrs. Granger have assigned the oral report to Nick?

3 Based on what you have read so far, how would you rate Mrs. Granger as a teacher? Support your answer with facts and reasons.

RESPONSE JOURNAL

Which person in your own life do you think is most like Nick? Explain.

Strategies Good Readers Use

FOCUS STRATEGY USE CONTEXT TO CONFIRM MEANING

Find the word *crimson* on page 4. Use clues in the sentence and what you know about embarrassment to define *crimson*. Then check your answer in a dictionary.

SKILLS IN CONTEXT

FOCUS SKILL   **TEXT STRUCTURE: COMPARE AND CONTRAST: VENN DIAGRAM**   Each character in *Frindle* has his or her unique qualities. Make a Venn diagram to compare and contrast Nick and Mrs. Granger.

What You Need

- paper
- pen or pencil
- compass

What to Do

1. Use a compass to draw a Venn diagram like the one below.
2. Label the left circle *Nick*, label the middle section *Nick and Mrs. Granger*, and label the right circle *Mrs. Granger*.
3. Revisit Chapters 1–5 to find information about how Nick and Mrs. Granger are alike and different.
4. Fill in the Venn diagram with the information you gather from the story.
5. Share your diagram with a classmate.

Here is a comparison to get you started:
Both Nick and Mrs. Granger are clever.

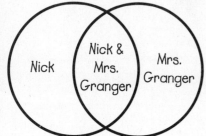

Think Ahead
Chapter 6 is titled "The Big Idea." What do you think the idea will be?

© Harcourt

Frindle

BOOK TALK

After you read Chapters 6–9, meet with your group to discuss and answer the following questions:

❶ How does learning about the dictionary lead Nick to invent the word *frindle*?

❷ If you were in Nick's class, would you use the word *frindle* even if you had to stay after school? Explain your point of view.

❸ What do you think will be in Mrs. Granger's letter? Explain.

RESPONSE JOURNAL

Do you think Mrs. Granger and Mrs. Chatham were right to make a school rule forbidding the use of the word *frindle*? Why or why not?

Strategies Good Readers Use

SUMMARIZE

*T*o make sure that you understand what you read, it is often helpful to summarize story events in your own words. Summarize Nick's *frindle* activity and the ways in which everyone responds to it.

SKILLS IN CONTEXT

NARRATIVE ELEMENTS: A NARRATIVE COMIC STRIP Think about the setting, characters, and plot of *Frindle*. Then work with a partner to create a comic strip about what you have learned about these narrative elements so far in Chapters 6–9.

What You Need

- pencils or markers
- paper
- a newspaper comics page for your reference

What to Do

1. Take notes on the setting, characters, and plot in Chapters 6–9.

2. Your comic strip will be divided into four panels. Decide which characters and events will be on each panel. Write words for the characters to say.

3. Illustrate each panel. Your background should reflect the setting, and your characters should look like their personalities.

4. Add words in speech balloons. Add color to your comic strip if you want to.

5. Present your comic strip to the class.

Here's an idea to get you started: *Nick invents the word* frindle.

Think Ahead
Who do you think will win the argument over the use of *frindle*?

Frindle

BOOK TALK

After you read Chapters 10–12, meet with your group
to discuss and answer the following questions:

1 How does reporter Judy Morgan help spread
the word about *frindle* to a national audience?

2 How do you know that Bud Lawrence is very successful in business?

3 Why do you think Nick's father decides to keep the contract a secret
from Nick?

RESPONSE JOURNAL

Do you think Nick enjoys talking about frindles on national television?
How would you have felt if you were Nick?

> ### Strategies Good Readers Use
>
> #### SELF-QUESTION
>
> Write one question
> that you asked your-
> self while reading
> Chapters 10–12. How
> did using this strategy
> help you to under-
> stand this part of the
> story?

SKILLS IN CONTEXT

TEXT STRUCTURE: CAUSE AND EFFECT: A CAUSE-AND-EFFECT FRINDLE CHAIN Keeping track
of the order of story events will help you understand the cause-and-effect relationships of certain events. The sequence of events can often form a cause-and-effect chain, in which each
event causes a new event to occur. Once Judy Morgan, a reporter for *The Westfield Gazette*,
learns about Nick's new word, amazing events begin to occur. Make a cause-and-effect chain
to show the sequence that unfolds.

What You Need

- scrap paper
- construction paper
- scissors
- glue or tape
- pencil (or frindle!)

What to Do

1. On scrap paper, list the sequence of events that occurs after Judy
Morgan's article appears in the newspaper. Think about whether
or not one event leads directly to another. Edit your list so that it
presents a clear chain of events.

2. Cut several horizontal strips from construction paper. Write one
event on each strip.

3. Use glue or tape to link the strips together to form a chain
that shows the correct sequence of causes and
effects.

Here is a short sequence to get you started:

*Judy writes her article. Alice Lunderson, who works at the local
CBS-TV station, reads the article and becomes interested in the story.*

Think Ahead
Do you think Nick will
get rich because of
the frindles?

© Harcourt

Frindle

BOOK TALK

Have students meet with their groups to discuss and answer the following questions:

1 What would you say is the most important message of this book? Why?

2 How does Nick's new word, *frindle*, change his life?

3 If Nick was a college student looking back on fifth grade, what words might he use to describe Mrs. Granger?

RESPONSE JOURNAL

How do you think Mrs. Granger feels when she learns that Nick has established a scholarship in her name? Explain.

Strategies Good Readers Use

FOCUS STRATEGY **USE CONTEXT TO CONFIRM MEANING**

Find the word *commotion* on page 93. Use clues in the paragraph, as well as your knowledge of story events, to define *commotion*. Check your answer in a dictionary.

SKILLS IN CONTEXT

FOCUS SKILL **TEXT STRUCTURE: COMPARE AND CONTRAST: MAKE A VENN DIAGRAM** Read Chapters 13–15 and look for elements in the story that you can compare and contrast. Then work with two classmates to make a Venn diagram.

What You Need

- **paper**
- **pen or pencil**
- **compass**

What to Do

1. Review pages 1–9 to find things to compare and contrast.
2. With your compass, draw two circles. The two circles should overlap one another.
3. In the left circle, write words that tell only about one thing. In another circle, write words that tell only about another thing. In the center section, write words that tell about both things.

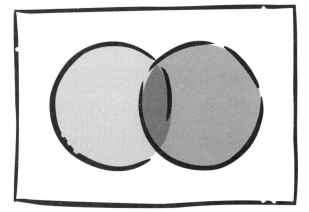

Here is an idea to get you started:
How was Nick's life before he invented the word frindle? *How was his life after?*

Wrap-Up

▶ **Project** **INVENT NEW WORDS** In *Frindle*, Nick invents the word *frindle* to mean "pen." Tell students that they will be inventing new words and creating an original dictionary with definitions for their words.

- Organize students into groups.
- Have students complete the copying master on page 107 to plan their words and dictionaries.
- Have students create an original dictionary.
- Have each group publish its dictionary and present it to the class.

▶ **Writing** **RESEARCH REPORT** Based on *Frindle* and related topics of classroom discussion, brainstorm with students a list of interesting topics for brief, four-paragraph research reports. Then have students respond to the following writing prompt: **Write a four-paragraph research report about a topic of your choosing.** Tell students to focus on organization. Have students use the copying master on page 108 to plan their research reports. Rubrics for evaluating student writing are provided on pages 154–157.

▶ **Language Link** **IMAGES** Have students reread Mrs. Granger's letter to Nick (pages 98–100). Point out that she uses the image of a sunrise. She compares the sunrise to Nick's "frindle" activity—something that can be watched but not slowed down or stopped. Ask students to think of other things that can be compared to a sunrise.

Inquiry Project

Frindle can be a springboard for inquiry into a variety of topics and ideas. Have students brainstorm topics they would like to know more about and organize their responses in a web. Students can use reference books and the Internet to begin their inquiry projects.

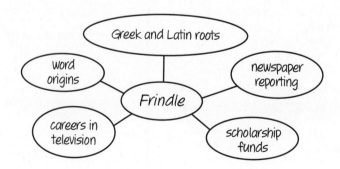

✔ **Comprehension Test** Test students' comprehension of *Frindle* by having them complete the copying master on page 109.

Project Planner

With Nick as your inspiration, create new words for the English language. Then work with your group to combine your new words to form an original dictionary.

☐ **Step 1.** Discuss with your group possible sources for new words. Be creative. Think of "make-believe" words you or a younger sister or brother might have used. Think of the names of characters from *Frindle*. Think of some of Nick's creative expressions, such as "thought-grenade" (page 15). Use the following lines to jot down your ideas.

_____ _____

_____ _____

_____ _____

What You Need
- Glossary, *Distant Voyages*
- index cards and pencils
- construction paper for cover of dictionary

☐ **Step 2.** Divide the list of words equally among group members. Work independently, and write each of your words at the top of an index card. Then, use the *Distant Voyages* Glossary as a model for drafting your dictionary entries. Write the entries on your cards. Include the part of speech, a definition, a model sentence, and one or more synonyms.

Word: judymorgan

Dictionary entry: noun A person who writes interesting news articles: The article about the baseball game was expertly written by a senior judymorgan at *The Gainsborough Times*. syn. journalist

☐ **Step 3.** Meet with your group to discuss, revise, and proofread all cards. Then put the cards in alphabetical order. Type or neatly print the entries to create the dictionary pages. Use construction paper to make a cover for your dictionary, and list all the literary staff members on it.

☐ **Step 4.** As a group, share a few sample entries from your dictionary.

Research Report

Write a four-paragraph research report about a topic of your choosing. As Nick did, support your topic by gathering accurate facts, details, and statistics. Once you have finished your research, use the graphic organizer below to plan your report.

Prewriting Graphic Organizer

Report Title: _____

Introduction

_____

_____

Body (at least two paragraphs)

_____

_____

_____

_____

_____

_____

_____

Conclusion

_____

_____

_____

Name _____

Comprehension Test

Test Prep

Read each question below. Then mark the letter for the answer you have chosen.

1. **Why does Mrs. Granger send a letter to the parents of her students?**
   - Ⓐ She wants to schedule conferences.
   - Ⓑ She wants every home to have a good dictionary.
   - Ⓒ She wants parents to help students with homework.
   - Ⓓ She wants to introduce herself.

2. **What is the subject of Nick's oral report?**
   - Ⓕ the history of pens
   - Ⓖ Latin and Greek root words
   - Ⓗ the dictionary
   - Ⓙ the English language

3. **What is a _frindle_?**
   - Ⓐ a pencil
   - Ⓑ a pen
   - Ⓒ a notebook
   - Ⓓ a measuring device

4. **What makes the fifth-grade class picture different that year?**
   - Ⓕ Each student wears a funny mask.
   - Ⓖ Each student waves at the camera.
   - Ⓗ No one smiles.
   - Ⓙ Each student holds up a frindle.

5. **Why doesn't Mrs. Granger give Nick the letter right away?**
   - Ⓐ She wants to be able to change it.
   - Ⓑ She wants to wait until the "word war" is over.
   - Ⓒ She wants to wait until Nick is in college.
   - Ⓓ She misplaces it.

6. **How does Judy Morgan help to bring attention to Nick and the word _frindle_?**
   - Ⓕ She gets a trademark for the word.
   - Ⓖ She tells her friends about the word.
   - Ⓗ She calls her friend who has a national television program.
   - Ⓙ She writes a newspaper article about Nick's new word.

7. **What does Nick's father do with Nick's share of the frindle profits?**
   - Ⓐ He sets up a trust account for Nick.
   - Ⓑ He improves the food at the cafeteria.
   - Ⓒ He starts a scholarship fund.
   - Ⓓ He buys Nick a mountain bike.

8. **Why does Mrs. Granger send Nick a dictionary?**
   - Ⓕ She wants to help him with his studies.
   - Ⓖ The dictionary is published by her students.
   - Ⓗ The dictionary contains many new words.
   - Ⓙ The dictionary contains the word _frindle_.

9. **What does Nick do to show his gratitude and affection for Mrs. Granger?**
   - Ⓐ He starts using the word _pen_ again.
   - Ⓑ He signs her dictionary.
   - Ⓒ He establishes a scholarship in her name.
   - Ⓓ He gives her a million dollars.

10. **Respond to the question below.**

    Do you think the word _frindle_ would have become as popular as it did if Mrs. Granger hadn't decided to fight against its use? Explain.

Beetles, Lightly Toasted

Reading Level

by Phyllis Reynolds Naylor

Author Profile

Former elementary school-teacher Phyllis Reynolds Naylor writes because she is curious about "what it would be like to be a preacher or a bicycle courier or a motherless twelve-year-old or a bridge worker." She has written more than fifty books for children and adults.

Additional Books by the Author
- *The Keeper*
- *The Agony of Alice*
- *Shiloh*

▶ **Theme Connection** As students read *Beetles, Lightly Toasted*, they will learn about a character who enters an annual fifth-grade essay contest. The main character, Andy, uses imagination to win a school competition and spark the interest of the community.

▶ **Summary** Ten-year-old Andy Moller is determined to win an essay contest offered to fifth graders. This year's topic—conservation—bores him until one day he watches a beetle and wonders if people could safely eat insects to supplement the food supply. After testing recipes on unsuspecting friends and family, he writes a winning essay. At the award ceremony, he pays the price for his experiments and has to eat his own culinary creations.

▶ **Building Background** Tell students that *Beetles, Lightly Toasted* is realistic fiction. Explain to them that this story features characters who might be similar to real people they know. The story is also set in modern times with events that occur in the real world. Encourage volunteers who have entered or won school contests to share their experiences. Then have students read to be entertained and to find out what happens when one fifth grader enters a contest at his school.

Vnvocabulary

H ave two teams of students play "Beetles." Give the first player of one team a vocabulary word from the list below. If the player defines it correctly, he or she draws one part of a beetle's body on the chalkboard. Alternate between the two teams until one team has completed a beetle. See pages 158–161 for additional vocabulary activities.

Day 1	Day 2	Day 3	Day 4
silo p. 3	conservation p. 26	listless p. 35	primitive p. 53
receptacle p. 5	boycott p. 26	repulsive p. 37	novelty p. 54
inventiveness p. 6	disgruntled p. 26	finicky p. 37	edible p. 57
			pupae p. 57
			entomologist p. 57

Day 5	Day 6	Day 7	Day 8
reproachfully p. 74	delirious p. 89	hearty p. 101	initiative p. 116
indignantly p. 76	queasy p. 89	memorializing p. 107	ingenuity p. 125
scrabbling p. 82	squishy p. 94		inquisitiveness p. 129

© Harcourt

	Response	Strategies	Skills
Day 1 Chapters 1–2	**Book Talk** • Characters' Traits • Characters' Emotions • Main Idea **Writing:** Express Personal Opinions	**ADJUST READING RATE** `FOCUS STRATEGY`	**AUTHOR'S PURPOSE AND PERSPECTIVE** `FOCUS SKILL` *Distant Voyages* pp. T532–T533
Day 2 Chapters 3–4	**Book Talk** • Characters' Emotions • Important Details • Make Predictions **Writing:** Express Personal Opinions	Summarize	Prefixes, Suffixes, and Roots *Distant Voyages* pp. T44–T45
Day 3 Chapters 5–6	**Book Talk** • Cause-Effect • Draw Conclusions • Make Predictions **Writing:** Express Personal Opinions	Create Mental Images	Draw Conclusions *Distant Voyages* pp. T160–T161
Day 4 Chapters 7–8	**Book Talk** • Important Details • Sequence • Make Judgments **Writing:** Characters' Emotions	**ADJUST READING RATE** `FOCUS STRATEGY`	**AUTHOR'S PURPOSE AND PERSPECTIVE** `FOCUS SKILL` *Distant Voyages* pp. T532–T533
Day 5 Chapters 9–10	**Book Talk** • Cause-Effect • Draw Conclusions • Important Details **Writing:** Compare and Contrast	Reread to Clarify	Graphic Aids *Distant Voyages* pp. T294–T295
Day 6 Chapters 11–12	**Book Talk** • Compare and Contrast • Make Comparisons • Draw Conclusions **Writing:** Personal Response	Use Context to Confirm Meaning	Text Structure: Compare and Contrast *Distant Voyages* pp. T510–T511
Day 7 Chapters 13–14	**Book Talk** • Sequence • Classify • Draw Conclusions **Writing:** Express Personal Opinions	Make and Confirm Predictions	Locate Information *Distant Voyages* pp. T623A–T623B
Day 8 Chapters 15–16	**Book Talk** • Make Comparisons • Theme • Make Judgments **Writing:** Write a Caption	Reread to Clarify	Graphic Aids *Distant Voyages* pp. T294–T295
Day 9 Wrap-Up	**Project** ✓ Create a Creepy Crawly Cookbook • Inquiry Project	**Writing** ✓ Research Report	**Language Link** • Cultural Foods **Assessment** ✓ Comprehension Test

*Additional support is provided in *Trophies*.
✓ Options for Assessment

Beetles, Lightly Toasted • 111

Beetles, Lightly Toasted

BOOK TALK

After you read Chapters 1 and 2, meet with your group to discuss and answer the following questions:

1 What does Andy's approach to his chores tell you about him?

2 How does Andy feel about the Roger B. Sudermann Contest?

3 Why does Andy feel this way about the contest?

RESPONSE JOURNAL

What do *you* think would make a good essay topic for the annual Roger B. Sudermann Contest?

Strategies Good Readers Use

FOCUS STRATEGY ADJUST READING RATE

Pay close attention to the speed at which you are reading Chapters 1–2. Make sure that your reading rate gives you enough time to identify and interpret important information and details in the story.

SKILLS IN CONTEXT

FOCUS SKILL AUTHOR'S PURPOSE AND PERSPECTIVE: AROUND THE TABLE An author's perspective is his or her opinion or attitude about a subject. To determine the author's perspective, you need to understand whether his or her purpose is writing to entertain, persuade, or inform. With a small group of classmates, hold a roundtable discussion about the author's purpose and perspective in Chapters 1 and 2 of *Beetles, Lightly Toasted*.

What You Need

- notebook paper
- writing materials
- tape recorder or video camera

What to Do

1. In your notebook, write your ideas about the author's purpose and perspective. Think about the author's opinions of Andy, contests, and the Mollers. Consider her purpose for expressing these opinions and the effects she wants to create.

2. Choose one group member to lead the discussion. Choose another to record it so that you can review points that were made or share your ideas with other groups.

3. Take turns expressing your views. Support your ideas with reasons and examples from the story.

4. Have the discussion leader summarize the main points discussed.

Here is a sentence you might use to determine the author's perspective on Andy: *"Andy had been writing down possible topics in the back of his old green notebook, ideas such as 'Could Human Beings Hibernate?' and 'How I Would Catch the Loch Ness Monster.'"*

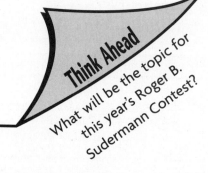

Think Ahead
What will be the topic for this year's Roger B. Sudermann Contest?

© Harcourt

Beetles, Lightly Toasted

BOOK TALK

After you read Chapters 3 and 4, meet with your group to discuss and answer the following questions:

1 How does Andy feel about the contest topic?

2 What strategy do Andy and his classmates decide to follow after Mrs. Haynes announces this topic?

3 Do you think the students' strategy will be successful? Why or why not?

RESPONSE JOURNAL

If you were in fifth grade at Bucksville Elementary, what topic related to conservation would you write about?

> **Strategies Good Readers Use**
>
> **SUMMARIZE**
>
> In your own words, tell a classmate three main events that take place in Chapters 3 and 4. Summarizing can help you understand and recall what you read.

SKILLS IN CONTEXT

PREFIXES, SUFFIXES, AND ROOTS: DON'T BUG ME Breaking an unfamiliar word into its parts can help you find word parts that are familiar. From these familiar word parts, you can often determine the word's meaning. A compound word combines two or more words (*mailbox = mail + box*). Other words combine a prefix or a suffix with a root word (*un + usual = unusual/excite + ment = excitement*). You will create bugs from word parts that you find in Chapters 3 and 4 of *Beetles, Lightly Toasted*.

What You Need

- **construction paper**
- **writing materials**
- **scissors**
- **chenille sticks**
- **glue**

What to Do

1. In Chapters 3 and 4, find two compound words, two words with prefixes, and two words with suffixes. Write each word on a slip of construction paper.

2. Draw a line between the parts of each word.

3. Use familiar word parts to determine the meaning of each word. Then cut each word into its parts.

4. Choose the most difficult word to make into a bug. Cut out the shape of an insect's body from construction paper and glue each part of your word on it.

5. Add construction-paper and chenille-stick details to create a real or imaginary bug.

6. Display your word bug in the classroom.

Here are two words from the story to get you started:

excitement = excite + ment **(base word with a suffix)**

notebook = note + book **(compound word)**

Think Ahead
Will Jack break the boycott?

Beetles, Lightly Toasted

BOOK TALK

After you read Chapters 5 and 6, meet with your
group to discuss and answer the following questions:

1 Why do Andy, Russ, and Dora decide
to give Jack the silent treatment?

2 Why does Andy want to keep the Soul Food Kitchen in business?

3 Do you think Andy will enter the essay contest? Why or why not?

RESPONSE JOURNAL

If you lived in Bucksville and wanted to eat out, where would you go—to the
pizza stand, the Home-Style Restaurant, or the Soul Food Kitchen and Carry-Out?

> **Strategies Good Readers Use**
>
> ### CREATE MENTAL IMAGES
>
> *A*s you read, note descriptive language that creates mental images. Sketch an image of a character or event from Chapters 5 and 6.

SKILLS IN CONTEXT

DRAW CONCLUSIONS: RESTAURANT FLYER Since writers do not always state things directly, you
may have to use the information that an author does give you to draw conclusions. To draw a
conclusion, you combine facts and details in the text with personal knowledge and experience
to make a logical statement about a topic. Andy thinks there are few decent places to eat
where he lives. Imagine that a new restaurant is about to open in Bucksville. The restaurant will
serve Andy's favorite dishes. Draw conclusions about a menu that would please Andy, and then
create a flyer to advertise this new restaurant.

What You Need

- **construction paper**
- **notebook paper**
- **writing materials**
- **typewriter or computer**

What to Do

1. Use facts and details from the story and your personal knowledge
   and experience to draw conclusions about the kinds of foods that
   Andy likes. Jot down your ideas on a sheet of paper.

2. Draft the text for a flyer. The purpose of your flyer is to advertise
   a new restaurant in Bucksville. The flyer should include an appropriate name, a list of featured dishes that Andy likes, and a
   catchy slogan. Use the example of a restaurant flyer on page 46
   for ideas.

3. Write or print the text of your flyer on a sheet of construction
   paper.

4. Display your flyer in the classroom.

*Here is a sentence from the story to help you draw
conclusions about foods Andy likes:* "Put a sausage pizza
in front of him right now, in fact, and he'd eat the whole thing."

Think Ahead
What terrific idea for an essay topic does Andy think of?

© Harcourt

Beetles, Lightly Toasted

BOOK TALK

After you read Chapters 7 and 8, meet with your group to discuss and answer the following questions:

1 What essay topic does Andy think of while watching a brown beetle?

2 What steps does Andy take to try out his idea?

3 Do you think Andy's essay topic is a good choice? Why or why not?

RESPONSE JOURNAL

How do you think Andy feels when he receives the letter from John Burrows?

Strategies Good Readers Use

FOCUS STRATEGY ADJUST READING RATE

Choose a paragraph from pages 53–65 and reread it twice—once at a faster pace than your usual reading rate, and once at a slower pace than your usual reading rate. Which pace do you feel more comfortable with?

SKILLS IN CONTEXT

FOCUS SKILL AUTHOR'S PURPOSE AND PERSPECTIVE: YOU'VE GOT MAIL An author's purpose, or reason for writing, may be to entertain, inform, or persuade. Knowing an author's perspective, or attitude about a subject, can help you determine his or her purpose for writing. With your group, create a chart to identify the purposes and perspectives of two letter writers.

What You Need

- **newspaper or magazine**
- **poster board**
- **colored markers**
- **ruler**

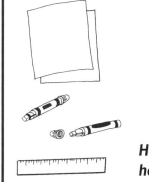

What to Do

1. Create a large chart like this one on poster board.

	Purpose	Perspective
John Burrow's letter		
Letter to the editor		

2. Reread the letter from John Burrows on page 57 of *Beetles, Lightly Toasted*. Identify his perspective and his main purpose for writing. Write your ideas on the chart.

3. Find and read a letter to the editor of a newspaper or magazine. Then identify the purpose and perspective of the letter writer. Write your ideas on the chart.

4. Share your chart with other groups.

Here is a sentence from the letter to help you identify the entomologist's perspective: "*Probably most insects are edible, especially their larvae or pupae.*"

Think Ahead How will Andy use the information that John Burrows provided?

Beetles, Lightly Toasted

BOOK TALK

After you read Chapters 9 and 10, meet with your group to discuss and answer the following questions:

1 What happens when Andy offers brownies to his classmates?

2 What do you think Jack plans to write about for the contest? Why do you think so?

3 What happens the day that Sam comes home with Andy?

RESPONSE JOURNAL

In what ways are the methods that Jack and Andy use to test their contest ideas similar? In what ways are their methods different?

SKILLS IN CONTEXT

GRAPHIC AIDS: FOOD FOR THOUGHT Paying attention to text features such as special type can help you better understand what an author wants to emphasize and how the text is organized. With a partner, create a chart of text features in Chapters 9 and 10.

What You Need

- notebook paper
- writing materials

What to Do

1. Create a chart like the one below on a sheet of paper.

Text Feature	Example	Page Number	Purpose
Italics			
Dashes			
Dots (ellipses)			
Dark type			

2. Fill in examples of each text feature in Chapters 9 and 10.

3. Discuss with your partner why you think the author used each text feature. Write your ideas in the last column of the chart.

4. Share your chart with other pairs of students to compare your findings.

Here is an example of italics found on page 66:
"*Why* wouldn't I want any?"

Think Ahead
What will happen when Sam helps Andy with a second food experiment?

© Harcourt

Beetles, Lightly Toasted

BOOK TALK

After you read Chapters 11 and 12, meet with your group to discuss and answer the following questions:

1 In what ways are the Mollers and the Hollinses alike? In what ways are the two families different?

2 How is Andy's second food experiment different from his first?

3 How do you know that Andy and Sam are good friends?

RESPONSE JOURNAL

What kind of friend do you think Andy would be? Would you want to be his friend? Why or why not?

Strategies Good Readers Use

USE CONTEXT TO CONFIRM MEANING

*W*rite two or three unfamiliar words that you encountered in Chapters 11 and 12. Then use context clues to determine the meaning of each word you listed.

SKILLS IN CONTEXT

TEXT STRUCTURE: COMPARE AND CONTRAST: PEAS IN A POD Comparing and contrasting helps you understand how certain story elements are alike or different. When Andy and Sam stay overnight at one another's houses, they discover how their lives are similar and different. You will use details in Chapters 11 and 12 of *Beetles, Lightly Toasted* to create a Venn diagram in which you show ways that Andy and Sam are alike and different.

What You Need

- **notebook paper**
- **writing materials**

What to Do

1. Look in Chapters 11 and 12 for details about how Andy and Sam are alike and different. Jot down your notes on notebook paper.

2. Copy this Venn diagram on a separate sheet of paper.

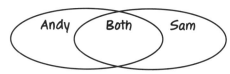

3. Use your notes to complete the Venn diagram. Write characteristics that both Andy and Sam share in the area labeled *Both*. Then write characteristics that are unique to Andy and Sam in the circles labeled *Andy* and *Sam*.

4. Share your Venn diagram with a small group of classmates.

Here is a detail from the story to get you started:
"Suppertime at the Hollins' was a lot later than it was at the Mollers'."

Think Ahead
Will Andy try different foods to see how they taste?

© Harcourt

Beetles, Lightly Toasted

BOOK TALK

After you read Chapters 13 and 14, meet with your group to discuss and answer the following questions:

1 What is the third thing Andy makes for the contest, and who tests it?

2 According to Andy's essay, what are two benefits of using insects as a source of food?

3 Why does Andy change his mind about winning the essay contest?

RESPONSE JOURNAL

Think about the essay topics that were chosen by Andy and Jack. Which essay would you prefer to read? Why?

Strategies Good Readers Use

MAKE AND CONFIRM PREDICTIONS

*W*rite down your prediction about who will win the Roger B. Sudermann essay contest. Then confirm or revise your prediction when you read Chapter 15.

SKILLS IN CONTEXT

LOCATE INFORMATION: INSECT INFORMATION, PLEASE Knowing how to use an encyclopedia can help you locate the information you need. When Andy needs one more thing to cook for his essay, he decides to look in an encyclopedia to find information about larvae and pupae. You will use an encyclopedia to locate information about an adult insect. Then you will create a fact sheet to share your findings.

What You Need

- **notebook paper**
- **writing and drawing materials**
- **encyclopedia in print, on CD-ROM, or on-line**

What to Do

1. Choose an insect you would like to research.

2. Use an encyclopedia to research the insect you choose. Jot down on a sheet of paper some interesting facts that you find.

3. Create a fact sheet by listing information about the insect you researched. Be sure to record unusual facts and details that will interest your classmates.

4. Add illustrations to your fact sheet, such as a diagram of the insect or a map to show where it is found.

5. Share your fact sheet with your classmates, or post it on an Insect Information bulletin board.

Here is information about ants that Andy locates in an encyclopedia: Worker ants can carry larvae or pupae in their jaws.

Think Ahead Will Andy's classmates and relatives discover the roles they played in Andy's experiments?

© Harcourt

Beetles, Lightly Toasted

BOOK TALK

After you read Chapter 15 and 16, meet with your group to discuss and answer the following questions:

❶ Which selection in *Distant Voyages* features events or characters that are similar to those in *Beetles, Lightly Toasted*? Explain.

❷ What lesson do you think Andy learns as a result of the essay contest?

❸ Do you agree with Andy's method of testing his essay contest ideas? Why or why not?

RESPONSE JOURNAL

Write a caption for one of the award ceremony photographs shot by the photographer from the *Bucksville Gazette.*

Strategies Good Readers Use

REREAD TO CLARIFY

Reading a passage again or going back to an earlier part of a story can help you understand what you are reading. Write down something that puzzled you as you read Chapters 15 and 16. Reread to help you figure it out.

SKILLS IN CONTEXT

GRAPHIC AIDS: LET'S DO LUNCH! Writers use graphic aids to emphasize ideas or highlight the way the text is organized. The *Bucksville Gazette* publishes an announcement about the award ceremony for the Roger B. Sudermann Contest. Write that announcement, adding text features to call attention to certain words, phrases, or sentences.

What You Need

- **notebook paper**
- **writing materials**
- **local newspaper**
- **computer and word processing software**

What to Do

1. Revisit Chapters 15 and 16 to review details about the award ceremony. Look closely at the passage on page 128 about the announcement in the *Bucksville Gazette.* Jot down answers to *who, what, where, when, why,* and *how* questions.

2. Study examples of newspaper announcements. Note the kinds of information that are included and how they are presented.

3. Draft your announcement. Include information telling *why, when, where, who,* and *what.*

4. Use a computer and word processing software to type the text of your announcement and apply text features to it.

5. Print your announcement and post it in the classroom.

Here is information from the story that you may use in your announcement: *"On June 10, Jack Barth and Andy Moller each will receive an award and a check from Luther Sudermann, publisher of the Bucksville Gazette, who organized the contest in memory of his son."*

Wrap-Up

> **Project** **CREATE A CREEPY CRAWLY COOKBOOK** Remind students that Andy tests some very unusual recipes before he writes his prizewinning essay. Tell them that they will write recipes that Andy might have used for his food experiments.
>
> - Organize students into small groups and have them discuss the information they need to include in a recipe.
> - Ask them to complete the copying master on page 121 to plan what recipes they will write and how to write them.
> - Have the class work together to create a cookbook.

> **Writing** **RESEARCH REPORT** Have students respond to the following writing prompt: **Write a research report about a recent or past invention that conserves time, energy, or natural resources.** Have students use the copying master on page 122 to plan their reports. Remind students to focus on organization, or relating ideas in a logical order. Rubrics for evaluating student writing are provided on pages 194–197.

> **Language Link** **CULTURAL FOODS** This story contains numerous references to foods that are enjoyed by people in different cultures and regions. Have students find different foods named in this story, such as sweet potato pie, okra, pizza, baked beans, wonton, and egg rolls. Then have them make a food "map" to show which cultures or regions—Chinese, African American, Southern United States, and so on—are associated with these foods.

Inquiry Project

Beetles, Lightly Toasted can spark interest in a variety of inquiry topics. Have students brainstorm topics and list them in a web or a chart similar to this one. Students can use reference books and the Internet to begin their inquiry projects.

	Beetles, Lightly Toasted
Biology	beetles, mealworm grubs, earthworms
Ecology	conservation
Chemistry	protein
Meteorology	weather forecasts

✔ **Comprehension Test** Test students' comprehension of *Beetles, Lightly Toasted* by having them complete the copying master on page 123.

Name _____

Project Planner

Using what you know about Andy's cooking experiences from reading the novel, write two recipes that Andy might have used for one of his food experiments. Then help create a class cookbook to share your recipes.

☐ **Step 1.** Discuss with your group the information usually found in a recipe. Make a list of ideas that your group will need to remember to include.

_____

_____

What You Need
- cookbooks
- index cards
- colored pencils and markers
- typewriter or computer
- construction paper
- plastic binder

☐ **Step 2.** Discuss with your group recipes that you would like to write. You may write Andy's recipes or invent original ones. If you invent your own recipes, you should consider the following questions:

- Are the insects I would like to use edible?
- Are the insects I would like to use easy to find?
- Will I be able to use these insects in a certain dish?

Create a chart similar to this one to brainstorm different recipes you might write.

Beetles	Earthworms	Grubs	Grasshoppers	Ants
Beetle Brownies	Deep-Fried Worms	Egg Salad with Grubs		

☐ **Step 3.** Choose two recipes from your chart. Then look at cookbooks to find out how to write a recipe. Notice the information that is provided as well as the format in which it is presented.

☐ **Step 4.** Write your recipes on index cards. Include a list of ingredients and numbered steps explaining how to make each dish. Be sure to define any unfamiliar terms or ingredients.

☐ **Step 5.** Work together as a class to create a cookbook. Use a typewriter or computer to publish each of the recipes you want to include. Then arrange recipes in alphabetical order or in categories such as main dish, appetizer, and dessert. Add a table of contents and a title. Draw illustrations of ingredients, steps in the process, or the finished products.

© Harcourt

Name _____

Research Report

Write a research report about a recent or past invention that conserves time, energy, or natural resources. Present ideas in a logical order, and include facts and details to make your sentences more interesting and informative. Use the graphic organizer below to plan your report. Then draft your report.

Prewriting Graphic Organizer

Title: _____

Introduction: _____

_____

_____

_____

Body (at least two paragraphs): _____

_____

_____

_____

_____

_____

Conclusion: _____

_____

_____

_____

© Harcourt

Name _____

Comprehension Test

Read each question below. Then mark the letter for the answer you have chosen.

1. **Who was Roger B. Sudermann?**

   Ⓐ a famous inventor

   Ⓑ the publisher of the *Bucksville Gazette*

   Ⓒ a fifth-grade student who died in a fall

   Ⓓ a teacher at Bucksville Elementary School

2. **What is the topic for this year's Roger B. Sudermann Contest?**

   Ⓕ cooking

   Ⓖ insects

   Ⓗ agriculture

   Ⓙ conservation

3. **To whom does Andy Moller turn for help with his idea?**

   Ⓐ Big Earl Moller

   Ⓑ Jack Barth

   Ⓒ Luther Sudermann

   Ⓓ John Burrows

4. **Which of the following insects does Andy *not* use in his experiments?**

   Ⓕ bees

   Ⓖ beetles

   Ⓗ grubs

   Ⓙ worms

5. **Which of the following characters does *not* try one of Andy's recipes?**

   Ⓐ Jack Barth

   Ⓑ Sam Hollins

   Ⓒ Aunt Wanda

   Ⓓ Lois Moller

6. **What is the result of Andy's experiments?**

   Ⓕ He finds out how to conserve water.

   Ⓖ He finds out that insects can be food.

   Ⓗ He learns to save energy while cooking.

   Ⓙ He finds out that garbage can be sent to outer space.

7. **Why is Andy afraid to win the contest?**

   Ⓐ He does not want to have his picture taken for the newspaper.

   Ⓑ He does not know what he will do with the prize money.

   Ⓒ His friends and family helped him.

   Ⓓ He does not want to hurt Jack's feelings.

8. **Who wins the contest?**

   Ⓕ Dora and Russ

   Ⓖ Andy and Dora

   Ⓗ Russ and Jack

   Ⓙ Jack and Andy

9. **Why does Andy agree to eat a "conservation lunch"?**

   Ⓐ to make up for what he has done

   Ⓑ to overcome his finicky food habits

   Ⓒ to help sell copies of the *Bucksville Gazette*

   Ⓓ to prove that his recipes are nutritious

10. **On a separate sheet of paper, write a short answer in response to the question below.**

    Why do you think Luther Sudermann chooses the winners he does for the annual Roger B. Sudermann Contest?

The Cat Who Escaped from Steerage

Reading Level

by Evelyn Wilde Mayerson

Theme Connection

As students read *The Cat Who Escaped from Steerage*, they will learn about a family that emigrates from Poland in 1910. The characters endure the hardships of a long ocean voyage on a crowded ship to explore a new life in America.

Summary

In 1910, nine-year-old Chanah and her family travel from Poland to America in the dirty, crowded steerage section of a ship. Chanah spends part of the journey searching for her cat; her family spends part of the journey worrying that cousin Yaacov, who is deaf, will not pass through Ellis Island. Happily, Yaacov is allowed to stay, and Chanah is reunited with her cat.

Author Profile

Evelyn Wilde Mayerson has taught psychiatry at Temple University and the University of South Florida at Tampa. She has also taught English at the University of Miami. She has written several adult novels, including *Miami: A Saga, Sanjo,* and *Well and Truly.*

Additional Books by the Author
• *Coydog: A Novel*

Building Background

Tell students that *The Cat Who Escaped from Steerage* is historical fiction about immigrants who sail to the United States. Explain that the story is set in the past and portrays events that possibly could have happened. Have students discuss the challenges faced by real-life immigrants they know or have read about. Then have students read to be entertained and to find out what happens to the immigrants in this book.

Vocabulary

Have pairs of students work together to role-play immigrants aboard a ship bound for America. Have them create and perform a dialogue in which they use the vocabulary words listed below. See pages 158–161 for additional vocabulary activities.

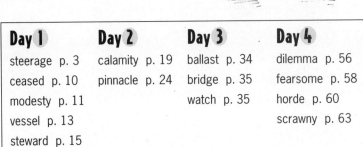

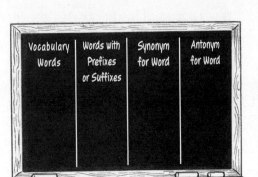

Vocabulary Words	Words with Prefixes or Suffixes	Synonym for Word	Antonym for Word

Day 1
steerage p. 3
ceased p. 10
modesty p. 11
vessel p. 13
steward p. 15

Day 2
calamity p. 19
pinnacle p. 24

Day 3
ballast p. 34
bridge p. 35
watch p. 35

Day 4
dilemma p. 56
fearsome p. 58
horde p. 60
scrawny p. 63

	Response	Strategies	Skills
Day 1 **Chapters 1–2**	**Book Talk** • Characters' Emotions • Generalize • Sequence **Writing:** Use Prior Knowledge	**SUMMARIZE** `FOCUS STRATEGY`	**TEXT STRUCTURE:** `FOCUS SKILL` **CAUSE AND** **EFFECT** *Distant Voyages* pp. T646–T647
Day 2 **Chapter 3**	**Book Talk** • Cause-Effect • Make Comparisons • Important Details **Writing:** Summarize	Create Mental Images	Text Structure: Compare and Contrast *Distant Voyages* pp. T510–T511
Day 3 **Chapters 4–5**	**Book Talk** • Cause-Effect • Important Details • Speculate **Writing:** Write a Diary Entry from Perspective of Character	Make and Confirm Predictions	Fact and Opinion *Distant Voyages* pp. T420–T421
Day 4 **Chapters 6–7**	**Book Talk** • Make Comparisons • Theme • Identify with Characters **Writing:** Speculate	**SUMMARIZE** `FOCUS STRATEGY`	**TEXT STRUCTURE:** `FOCUS SKILL` **CAUSE AND** **EFFECT** *Distant Voyages* pp. T646–T647
Day 5 **Wrap-Up**	**Project** ✓ Create a Bulletin Board Display • Inquiry Project **Writing** ✓ Rhymed Poem **Language Link** • Sensory Words **Assessment** ✓ Comprehension Test		

*Additional support is provided in *Trophies*.
✓ Options for Assessment

The Cat Who Escaped from Steerage • 125

The Cat Who Escaped from Steerage

BOOK TALK

After you read Chapters 1 and 2, meet with your group to discuss and answer the following questions:

1 How does Chanah's family feel about traveling to America in steerage?

2 Based on what you have read, how would you describe the conditions in steerage?

3 What happens after Chanah discovers that Pitsel is missing?

RESPONSE JOURNAL

How are Chanah's experiences of traveling from Poland to America in the early 1900s similar to or different from those of immigrants you know or have read about?

Strategies Good Readers Use

FOCUS STRATEGY   **SUMMARIZE**

Choose one event or idea from pages 1–18 and write a one-sentence summary. How does summarizing help you better understand the event or idea?

SKILLS IN CONTEXT

FOCUS SKILL   **TEXT STRUCTURE: CAUSE AND EFFECT: A STACK OF CAUSES** Cause-and-effect relationships show how an event (a cause) makes something else happen (an effect). Revisit Chapters 1–2 and look for cause-and-effect relationships. Then create a cause-and-effect game.

What You Need

- index cards or paper cut into squares
- writing tools

What to Do

1. Find five examples of cause-and-effect relationships in Chapters 1–2.

2. Write each of the six causes on six Cause cards. Write the six effects on six Effect cards.

3. Play the game with three classmates. Shuffle the Cause cards and place them in a stack in the center of the table. Shuffle the Effect cards and deal them to the players.

4. Each player in turn draws from the Cause card stack. If a player is holding a matching Effect card, the two cards are placed face up on the table. If not, the Cause card is placed face down beside the stack on the table.

5. Continue playing until all of the Cause and Effect cards have been matched.

Here is an example to get started: *Because the conditions in steerage were so uncomfortable, everyone tried to make the most of it.*

Think Ahead What will Chanah do to get her cat back?

The Cat Who Escaped from Steerage

BOOK TALK

After you read Chapter 3, meet with your group to discuss and answer the following questions:

1 How do the steerage passengers react during the storm, and why do they react this way?

2 Chanah and Yaacov search throughout the ship for Pitsel. How do the passenger accommodations they observe in other parts of the ship differ from those in steerage?

3 What plan do the steerage passengers make in order to get fresh water?

Strategies Good Readers Use

CREATE MENTAL IMAGES

Write down three descriptive details in Chapter 3 that help you picture in your mind what you read. Creating mental images as you read can help you understand and enjoy a selection.

RESPONSE JOURNAL

What challenges do immigrants in this story face during their journey to America?

SKILLS IN CONTEXT

TEXT STRUCTURE: COMPARE AND CONTRAST: STEAMSHIP BROCHURE When you compare two or more ideas, events, or characters, you show how they are similar. When you contrast two or more ideas, events, or characters, you show how they are different. Chanah and her family travel to America aboard the newest model steamship on the line. Create a steamship brochure in which you compare and contrast passengers' accommodations on the ship.

What You Need

- **notebook paper**
- **construction paper**
- **writing and drawing materials**

What to Do

1. Revisit Chapters 1 and 2 to review what steerage is like. Then review Chapter 3 to find out what Chanah and Yaacov discover about other parts of the ship when they leave steerage to search for Pitsel. Jot down details about each area on a sheet of paper.

2. Fold a sheet of construction paper into a brochure. Using your notes, write brief descriptions in your brochure to explain the different types of accommodations that are available on the ship.

3. Use details from the story to draw illustrations of steerage, the first-class deck, and the third-class deck. Add them to your brochure.

Here is information from Chapter 3 that you may use in your brochure: *"Surprises everywhere made them stare in wonder, such as floor-to-ceiling mirrors, doorways with portieres of crimson velvet, music rooms with draped pianos, floors made of tiny bits of marble . . .*

Think Ahead Why does the captain visit the passengers in steerage?

© Harcourt

The Cat Who Escaped from Steerage

BOOK TALK

After you read Chapters 4 and 5, meet with your group to discuss and answer the following questions:

1 Why does the captain visit the steerage hold?

2 How do the ship's officers figure out Yaacov's secret?

3 How do you think the immigrants feel as the ship sails into New York?

RESPONSE JOURNAL

Imagine that you are Chanah. Write a diary entry about your arrival in America. Use some of the vocabulary words in your entry.

Strategies Good Readers Use

MAKE AND CONFIRM PREDICTIONS

*W*rite down your predictions about whether Chanah will be reunited with Pitsel and, if so, how. Then confirm or revise your predictions when you read Chapters 6 and 7.

SKILLS IN CONTEXT

FACT AND OPINION: SHIP'S LOG ENTRY A fact is an idea that can be proven. An opinion is an idea that is a personal belief and cannot be proven. Opinions can vary from person to person. Imagine that you are a member of the crew or the captain in this story. You keep a ship's log, or a written record of the ship's speed and progress as well as of any important shipboard events. You will write an entry that includes facts and opinions from Chapters 4 and 5.

What You Need

- **notebook paper**
- **construction paper**
- **writing and drawing materials**

What to Do

1. Work in a small group. Each group member picks an event or events from Chapters 1–4 to write an entry about.

2. List facts and opinions that you will include in your log entry.

3. Write your ship's log entry on a clean sheet of paper. Add facts from the book and your own opinions.

4. Work with your group members to combine your entries into a ship's log. Arrange the entries in chronological order. Use construction paper and markers to create an illustrated cover.

5. Trade logs with another group. Identify facts and opinions in the logbook your group receives.

Here are a fact and an opinion from the story to get you started: *The captain christens a baby born aboard the ship. (fact) The German father is proud of his daughter. (opinion)*

Think Ahead
What do you think will happen to Yaacov when Ellis Island inspectors examine him?

© Harcourt

BOOK TALK

After you read Chapters 6 and 7, meet with your group to discuss and answer the following questions:

1 Which character in *Distant Voyages* experiences a journey that is most like the one Chanah takes to America?

2 What message about immigrants do you think the author conveys?

3 If you were an immigrant like Chanah, which would you dislike most—traveling in steerage or being examined at Ellis Island? Why?

RESPONSE JOURNAL

What do you think will happen to Chanah and her family now that they have finally arrived in America?

Strategies Good Readers Use

FOCUS STRATEGY **SUMMARIZE**
*R*eread chapters 6–7 and choose a character to write a short summary about. How does summarizing this character help you get to know him or her better?

SKILLS IN CONTEXT

FOCUS SKILL **TEXT STRUCTURE: CAUSE AND EFFECT: CAUSE-AND-EFFECT CHAIN** A cause is an event that makes something happen. An effect is what happens as a result of a cause. Causes can have several effects. Recognizing cause-and-effect relationships can help you better understand what you read. Make a chain to show the different cause-and-effect relationships in Chapters 6–7.

What You Need

- **notebook paper**
- **writing materials**
- **construction paper**
- **scissors**
- **glue or stapler**

What to Do

1. Look in Chapters 6 and 7 of *The Cat Who Escaped from Steerage* for cause-and-effect relationships. Jot them down on a sheet of paper.

2. Choose one cause-and-effect relationship that consists of a single cause and three or more effects.

3. Cut long strips of construction paper. Write the cause on one strip of paper. Write the effects on the other strips of paper. Use one color for the cause and another color for all of the effects.

4. Create a paper chain by either gluing or stapling interlocking strips of paper. String your paper chain in the classroom.

Here are a cause and an effect to get started:
Yonkel and his family waited underneath the pier because the docks of New York City were confusing.

Wrap-Up

▶ **Project** CREATE A BULLETIN BOARD DISPLAY Remind students that Chanah and her family emigrate from Poland to America in 1910. Tell them that they will research immigration and then create an informative bulletin board display to help them learn more about Chanah's experience.

- Organize students into small groups, and have them discuss what they would like to know about immigration in the early 1900s.
- Ask them to complete the copying master on page 131 to plan what facts and details they will share with the class.
- Then have each group contribute information to make a collaborative classroom display.

▶ **Writing** RHYMED POEM Have students respond to the following writing prompt: **Write a rhymed poem about a real or imaginary journey that you or someone you have read about has taken.** Have students use the copying master on page 132 to plan their poems. Remind students to focus on word choice. You can find rubrics for evaluating student writing on pages 154–157.

▶ **Language Link** SENSORY WORDS Sensory words tell how things look, sound, smell, feel, and taste. Writers use sensory words to bring their descriptions to life. Have students create a chart with these headings: *Sight, Hearing, Taste, Smell,* and *Touch.* Then have students record sensory words and images from *The Cat Who Escaped from Steerage* that helped them picture the setting of the story.

Inquiry Project

The Cat Who Escaped from Steerage can be a rich source of topics and ideas for inquiry. Have students brainstorm topics that they would like to know more about, and record their ideas in a word web like this one. Encourage students to use reference books and the Internet to begin their inquiry projects. You may wish to tie in several of the students' inquiry projects with their wrap-up project.

✔ **Comprehension Test** Test students' comprehension of *The Cat Who Escaped from Steerage* by having them complete the copying master on page 133.

Name _____

Project Planner

In *The Cat Who Escaped from Steerage*, Chanah and her family leave Poland in 1910 and sail to America to start a new life. Using what you learned from reading this story and from additional research, create a bulletin board display about immigration in the late 1800s and early 1900s.

☐ **Step 1.** Discuss with your group what kinds of information your display might feature.

☐ **Step 2.** As a group, discuss what you learned about immigration from reading *The Cat Who Escaped from Steerage*. Use the graphic organizer below.

What You Need
- construction paper
- drawing materials
- ruler
- scissors
- reference sources

Questions	Answers
1. How much did a steerage ticket cost?	
2. How many immigrants came to America in the late 1800s and early 1900s?	
3. Which countries did these immigrants come from?	

☐ **Step 3.** As a group, decide which reference sources to use to research immigration. Then decide how to present your information to the class.

☐ **Step 4.** Create bar graphs, pie graphs, time lines, and other graphic aids. Make photocopies of photographs and artifacts related to immigration in the late 1800s and early 1900s.

☐ **Step 5.** As a class, arrange each group's information on a bulletin board to create an informational display. Include descriptive labels and chart titles.

© Harcourt

Rhymed Poem

On a separate sheet of paper, write a rhymed poem about a real or imaginary journey that you or someone you have read about has taken. Before you begin, complete the word web below to brainstorm sensory images that will create a vivid picture of the journey in readers' minds. When you write your poem, choose a rhyming pattern for the lines and arrange the lines in stanzas.

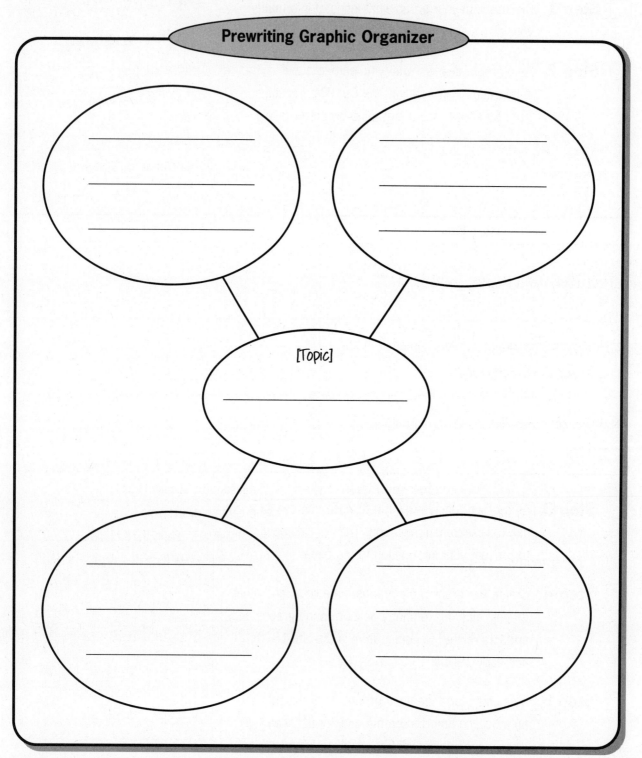

Prewriting Graphic Organizer

[Topic]

Name _____

Comprehension Test

Read each question below. Then mark the letter for the answer you have chosen.

1. **In which country does Chanah acquire Pitsel?**
   - Ⓐ Russia
   - Ⓑ Poland
   - Ⓒ America
   - Ⓓ France

2. **Why do Chanah and Yaacov leave steerage?**
   - Ⓕ to get fresh water to drink
   - Ⓖ to visit friends on the first-class deck
   - Ⓗ to search for the missing cat
   - Ⓙ to avoid the ship's captain

3. **How would you describe the accommodations observed by Chanah and Yaacov elsewhere on the ship?**
   - Ⓐ crowded
   - Ⓑ dirty
   - Ⓒ modest
   - Ⓓ luxurious

4. **Where do Chanah and Yaacov find Pitsel?**
   - Ⓕ dog kennel
   - Ⓖ tennis court
   - Ⓗ boiler room
   - Ⓙ cargo hold

5. **What sound indirectly reveals Yaacov's deafness to the ship's officers?**
   - Ⓐ footsteps
   - Ⓑ ship's bell
   - Ⓒ foghorn
   - Ⓓ gun salute

6. **Where do Chanah and her family go after their ship arrives in America?**
   - Ⓕ New Jersey
   - Ⓖ Ellis Island
   - Ⓗ New York City
   - Ⓙ Philadelphia

7. **What happens to Chanah and her family after their inspection?**
   - Ⓐ They receive landing cards.
   - Ⓑ They arc denied permission to enter the United States.
   - Ⓒ Chanah's parents are sent back to Poland.
   - Ⓓ They take a ferry directly to New Jersey.

8. **Why does the inspector let Yaacov stay?**
   - Ⓕ He is a personal friend of the family.
   - Ⓖ He accepts Chanah's appeal.
   - Ⓗ He does not realize that Yaacov is deaf.
   - Ⓙ He misunderstands the interpreter.

9. **Who gives Pitsel back to Chanah?**
   - Ⓐ the inspector at Ellis Island
   - Ⓑ the captain of the ship
   - Ⓒ the Polish woman in third class
   - Ⓓ the German couple in steerage

10. **On a separate sheet of paper, write a short answer in response to the question below.**

    What are two facts about immigration that you learned from reading this historical book?

And Then What Happened, Paul Revere?

Reading Level

by Jean Fritz

Theme Connection

In *And Then What Happened, Paul Revere?* students will meet an important figure of the American Revolution through an exploration in time.

Summary

In an exciting, fast-paced, and often humorous way, author Jean Fritz chronicles the life and adventures of Boston silversmith and patriot Paul Revere. With emphasis on Revere's famous ride on April 18, 1775, Fritz presents many interesting facts and details that enliven the history and make Revere a dynamic, accessible figure.

Building Background

Ask students to brainstorm facts they already know about Paul Revere. List their ideas on chart paper. Then explain that they will be reading *And Then What Happened, Paul Revere?*, a book that will probably give them information they did not already know about this famous American. Invite students to add new facts to the chart as they read. Have them read to be informed about Paul Revere's life.

Author Profile

Jean Fritz has written several children's books on famous Americans from the Revolutionary period. She has also written picture books for younger readers, as well as an adult novel entitled *Cast for a Revolution.*

Additional Books by the Author

- *Why Don't You Get a Horse, Sam Adams?*
- *Shh! We're Writing the Constitution*
- *Will You Sign Here, John Hancock?*

Vocabulary

Help students use the vocabulary words to create crossword puzzles like the one below. To create a puzzle, have students write selected words on graph paper, one letter per space, so the words interlock. Once they have found a pattern that includes all the words, have them number the words and write clues. Then have them create blank versions of the puzzles to exchange and solve. See pages 158–161 for additional vocabulary activities.

Day 1
vendors p. 7
wares p. 7
silversmithing p. 8
clapped p. 10
bookplates p. 14

Day 2
oppose p. 18
lampblack p. 18
patrolled p. 22
sentries p. 23

Day 3
dispatched p. 25
launched p. 30
volley p. 35

Day 4
succession p. 41
occupied p. 42
foundry p. 43

	Response	Strategies	Skills
Day 1 Pages 5–17	**Book Talk** • Important Details • Drawing Conclusions • Characters' Traits **Writing:** Compare and Contrast	**SELF-QUESTION** FOCUS STRATEGY	**CONNOTATION/ DENOTATION** FOCUS SKILL *Distant Voyages* pp. T622–T623
Day 2 Pages 18–23	**Book Talk** • Characters' Motivations • Draw Conclusions • Cause-Effect **Writing:** Write a Journal Entry from Character's Perspective	Read Ahead	Summarize and Paraphrase *Distant Voyages* pp. T182–T183
Day 3 Pages 24–35	**Book Talk** • Summarize • Cause-Effect • Draw Conclusions **Writing:** Personal Response	Reread to Clarify	Author's Purpose and Perspective *Distant Voyages* pp. T532–T533
Day 4 Pages 36–45	**Book Talk** • Compare and Contrast • Make Judgments • Make Inferences **Writing:** Express Personal Opinions	**SELF-QUESTION** FOCUS STRATEGY	**CONNOTATION/ DENOTATION** FOCUS SKILL *Distant Voyages* pp. T622–T623
Day 5 Wrap-Up	**Project** ✓ Create a Slide Show • Inquiry Project **Writing** ✓ News Story **Language Link** • "Old-Time" Words **Assessment** ✓ Comprehension Test		

*Additional support is provided in *Trophies*.
✓ Options for Assessment

© Harcourt

And Then What Happened, Paul Revere?

BOOK TALK

After you read pages 5–17, meet with your group to discuss and answer the following questions:

1. What was the city of Boston like in 1735?

2. Why were church bells important during colonial times?

3. Based on what you have read, what kind of person was Paul Revere?

RESPONSE JOURNAL

Think about how Boston is described in the book. Write a journal entry that compares Boston at that time to the community where you live.

Strategies Good Readers Use

FOCUS STRATEGY SELF-QUESTION

Based on what you have read so far, is Paul Revere someone you would like to know? Ask yourself questions like these as you continue reading and learning more about the characters.

SKILLS IN CONTEXT

FOCUS SKILL **CONNOTATION/DENOTATION: MAKE A CHART** The denotation of a word is its dictionary definition. The connotation of a word refers to the feelings and ideas that the word suggests to readers. Writers choose words for both their denotations and their connotations. Revisit *And Then What Happened, Paul Revere?* to look for words that give certain connotations.

What You Need

- **dictionary**
- **pen or pencil**
- **paper**

What to Do

1. Revisit pages 5–17 of *And Then What Happened, Paul Revere?* to find words that connote different meanings.

2. Make a chart like the one below. In the left column, write the word. In the middle column, write what feelings and ideas the words suggest to readers. (connotation) In the right column, write the dictionary definition of the words. (denotation)

3. Share your chart with a classmate. Discuss why you chose the connotations you did. If your classmate doesn't agree with your connotation, discuss reasons why, and what feelings and ideas he or she would choose to discuss instead.

Here are some words to get you started: cared, crying, ringing, polishing

Word	Connotation	Denotation

Think Ahead
What do you think Paul Revere did about the English tax on tea?

And Then What Happened, Paul Revere?

BOOK TALK

After you read pages 18–23, meet with your group to discuss and answer the following questions:

1 Why did the Sons of Liberty dump tea into Boston Harbor?

2 In your opinion, why did the Sons of Liberty decide to make Paul Revere their Number One express rider?

3 How did Paul Revere's life change because of the threat of war with England?

RESPONSE JOURNAL

Imagine that you are one of Paul Revere's children. Write a journal entry that explains how you feel about your father's opposition to the English.

Strategies Good Readers Use

READ AHEAD

*P*redict something that you think might happen in the next chapter of this book. Then read ahead to find out whether your prediction was correct.

SKILLS IN CONTEXT

SUMMARIZE AND PARAPHRASE: IN SO MANY WORDS Summarizing text means stating the most important ideas and leaving out unnecessary details. Paraphrasing means writing ideas in your own words. Play a game that challenges you to turn a long section of text into a short one—without leaving out the most important information!

What You Need

- notebook paper
- writing materials
- timer

What to Do

1. Select four or five paragraphs of text. Each section should be at least five lines long. Record the location of each paragraph; for example, "Page 18, paragraph 2."

2. Set the timer for one minute. Then have each member of your group summarize the first paragraph on your list in one complete sentence.

3. Read your summaries aloud. Then count the words. Give yourself one point for each word. The object is to have the fewest points.

4. Continue with the other paragraphs your group selected.

Here is a summary to get you started:
On December 16, 1773, the Sons of Liberty disguised themselves as Indians. (page 18, paragraph 2)

Think Ahead
What did Paul Revere do after he was freed?

© Harcourt

And Then What Happened, Paul Revere?

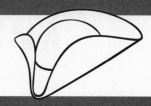

BOOK TALK

After you read pages 24–35, meet with your group to discuss and answer the following questions:

1 What was the reason for Paul Revere's "Big Ride"?

2 Why was it a lucky mistake that Paul left the door open so his dog could get out?

3 Why did the English officers want to keep Paul Revere as a prisoner?

RESPONSE JOURNAL

Paul Revere knew that riding out to give the alarm was a dangerous job, but he did it anyway. Write a journal entry about a time when you did something even though you were afraid or nervous about doing it.

> **Strategies Good Readers Use**
>
> **REREAD TO CLARIFY**
>
> ☆ One strategy good readers use is to reread sections they don't understand the first time. Describe one section of text that you reread. How did this strategy help you understand the text?

SKILLS IN CONTEXT

AUTHOR'S PURPOSE AND PERSPECTIVE: THAT'S ENTERTAINMENT! Authors have many reasons for writing. They may want to share information, to express personal opinions, to persuade others, or to entertain. The author of *And Then What Happened, Paul Revere?* wants to inform her readers about Paul Revere, but she also wants to entertain them. Identify examples of both of these purposes.

What You Need

- notebook paper cut into strips
- markers and other writing materials
- paper lunch bag
- large sheet of paper
- tape

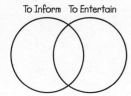

To Inform   To Entertain

What to Do

1. Work in a group. Look through the book for sentences that inform and sentences that entertain. Write each example on a strip of paper. Fold the strips and put them in the paper bag.

2. Draw two large overlapping circles on the sheet of paper. Label one circle *To Inform* and the other *To Entertain*.

3. Take turns pulling a slip of paper out of the bag. Tape the strip in the circle that identifies its purpose. If a sentence was written both to inform and to entertain, put it in the overlapping section of the circles.

Here is a sentence to get you started:
Paul gave directions to hang two lanterns in the steeple. (to inform)

Think Ahead
What will Paul Revere and John Hancock do about the trunk?

© Harcourt

And Then What Happened, Paul Revere?

BOOK TALK

After you read pages 36–45, meet with your group to discuss and answer the following questions:

1 What selections from *Distant Voyages* remind you of characters or events in *And Then What Happened, Paul Revere?*

2 Do you think Paul Revere was a brave man? Support your answer with details from the book.

3 What do you think was Paul Revere's greatest contribution to America's independence? Explain your answer.

RESPONSE JOURNAL

Would you have volunteered to join Paul Revere on his ride? Write a journal entry that explains your response.

Strategies Good Readers Use

FOCUS STRATEGY SELF-QUESTION

*W*hat questions have you asked yourself while reading this book? Think back to these questions and try to answer some of them, using new information you learned from pages 36–45.

SKILLS IN CONTEXT

FOCUS SKILL CONNOTATION/DENOTATION: HOW CONNOTATIONS CHANGE Remember that the connotation of a word refers to the feelings and ideas the word suggests to readers. The connotation of a word can change, depending on whether it is read in the context of the story or out of the context of the story.

What You Need

- **pen or pencil**
- **notebook paper**

Here are some words to get you started: *softly, signal, firing, store*

What to Do

1. Skim pages 36–45 of the book. On notebook paper, list words that give positive connotations. These words should make you feel good about something.

2. Next to each word, list reasons why you feel that it gives a positive connotation.

3. On another piece of paper, list words you find on those same pages that give negative connotations.

4. Next to each word, list reasons why you feel that it gives a negative connotation.

5. Take both pieces of paper and review your lists. Then find where each word appears in the book. If you read them in the context of the story, do they still make you feel positive or negative? Discuss with a teacher what you have learned about the connotations of words when they are used in context of the story, and when they are used out of context of the story.

Wrap-Up

> **Project** **CREATE A SLIDE SHOW** Remind students that one of the author's purposes for writing *And Then What Happened, Paul Revere?* was to inform her readers about Paul Revere and his accomplishments. Invite them to create a "slide show" that can be used to teach younger children about this famous American. Arrange students into small groups.
>
> • Have them complete the copying master on page 141 to plan their slide shows.
> • Have them present their shows to children in a younger grade.

> **Writing** **NEWS STORY** Have students respond to the following writing prompt: **Imagine that you are a news reporter for a colonial newspaper. Write a story about Paul Revere's ride.** Have students use the copying master on page 142 to plan their news stories. Remind students to focus on organization. Rubrics for evaluating student writing are provided on pages 154–157.

> **Language Link** **"OLD-TIME" WORDS** Explain to students that the author uses some words and phrases that are unfamiliar to readers today because they are no longer used or are used differently. Have students suggest several examples from the book. Then list them on the board and rewrite each in "modern" English.

Inquiry Project

And Then What Happened, Paul Revere? can be a springboard for inquiry into many areas. Have students brainstorm a list of topics. Then invite them to use reference books, the Internet, and CD-ROMs to find information on topics that most interest them. As appropriate, help students organize what they learn on a chart like the one shown below.

✔ **Comprehension Test** Test students' comprehension of *And Then What Happened, Paul Revere?* by having them complete the copying master on page 143.

Name _____

Project Planner

Use what you learned by reading *And Then What Happened, Paul Revere?* to teach younger students about this great American. Create a slide show of Paul Revere's accomplishments.

☐ **Step 1.** Decide with your group what events you want to show. In the boxes below, make notes and drawings to show what each "slide" will include.

What You Need

- several sheets of plain white paper
- markers
- notebook paper and pencil

Slide 1

Slide 2

Slide 3

Slide 4

Slide 5

Slide 6

☐ **Step 2.** Use a blank sheet of paper and markers to draw a scene for each slide. Use another sheet to create a title slide. Include the names of everyone in the group as authors of the show.

☐ **Step 3.** Decide what the narration will be for each slide. Record the narration on notebook paper and choose a narrator.

☐ **Step 4.** Put the slides in order. Then present the slides to an audience of younger students.

© Harcourt

Name _____

News Story

Imagine that you are a reporter for a colonial newspaper. Write a story about Paul Revere's ride. Use the organizer below to plan your news story.

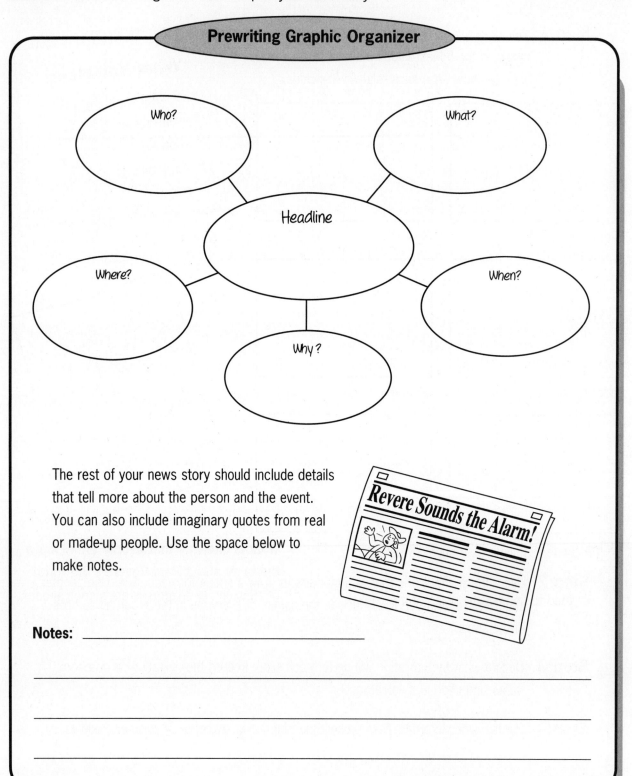

Prewriting Graphic Organizer

Who? What? Headline Where? When? Why?

The rest of your news story should include details that tell more about the person and the event. You can also include imaginary quotes from real or made-up people. Use the space below to make notes.

Revere Sounds the Alarm!

Notes: _____

_____

_____

_____

Name _____

Comprehension Test Test Prep

Read each question below. Then mark the letter for the answer you have chosen.

1. **Why did the colonists fight against the French and the Indians?**
   - Ⓐ The colonies had a treaty with them.
   - Ⓑ The colonists wanted to be part of France.
   - Ⓒ The French and the Indians were friends.
   - Ⓓ The French and the Indians were attacking the borders of the colonies.

2. **What mistake did Paul Revere once make?**
   - Ⓕ He made false teeth for a hippopotamus.
   - Ⓖ He added up numbers too fast.
   - Ⓗ He built a barn in the wrong place.
   - Ⓙ He forgot to put a spout on a teapot.

3. **Why did some colonists form a club called the Sons of Liberty?**
   - Ⓐ They thought a club would be interesting.
   - Ⓑ They wanted to work against the English.
   - Ⓒ They wanted to pretend to be Indians.
   - Ⓓ They wanted a place to go after work.

4. **As a special agent Paul Revere**
   - Ⓕ worked as a sentry.
   - Ⓖ rode to Philadelphia once a week.
   - Ⓗ made things from silver and gold.
   - Ⓙ tried to find out the plans of the English.

5. **Which of the following was NOT a clue that the English were ready to start fighting?**
   - Ⓐ A stableboy overheard their plans.
   - Ⓑ Boats had been moving English troops.
   - Ⓒ English soldiers questioned Paul Revere.
   - Ⓓ English scouts had been seen heading to Lexington and Concord.

6. **Why did the English officers take Paul Revere's horse?**
   - Ⓕ They did not want him to be able to warn the colonists.
   - Ⓖ They did not want to take prisoners.
   - Ⓗ They needed more horses.
   - Ⓙ Paul Revere had stolen the horse.

7. **What was important about the battles of Lexington and Concord?**
   - Ⓐ They were the deadliest battles of the Revolutionary War.
   - Ⓑ They marked the beginning of the war.
   - Ⓒ They made Paul Revere famous.
   - Ⓓ They were the biggest battles of the war.

8. **What was one job Paul Revere had after the Revolutionary War?**
   - Ⓕ He was a sentry for the army.
   - Ⓖ He wrote newspaper articles.
   - Ⓗ He made church bells.
   - Ⓙ He opened a clothing store.

9. **What is one way that people today know the facts about Paul Revere's Big Ride?**
   - Ⓐ Boston newspapers wrote stories about it.
   - Ⓑ Paul Revere wrote out the story of his ride.
   - Ⓒ Someone interviewed Paul Revere.
   - Ⓓ John Hancock wrote a book about the ride.

10. **Respond to the following question:**
    Why did colonists dress up like Indians and dump tea into Boston Harbor?

～Literature Circle Student Record～

STUDENT'S NAME _____ **DATE** _____

TITLE _____ **AUTHOR** _____

Use the following matrix to rate student behaviors as you observe students in Literature Circles. Use the information to assess skills and to identify areas where students may require additional support.

The Student	Often	Occasionally	Rarely
prepares for discussion			
participates in discussion			
offers quality responses to literature			
uses prior knowledge			
connects selection to real life and to other literature			
appreciates illustrations and uses graphic aids			
demonstrates use of listening skills through interaction and responses			
is willing to consider alternative viewpoints			
is willing to ask questions and seek help from others			
enjoys the literature			
Other Criteria: _____ _____ _____			

© Harcourt

Literature Circle Bookmarks

Cut out the bookmarks that go with the type of book you are reading. Use the questions on the bookmarks to help you remember things you might want to discuss in your literature circle group. On the backs of the bookmarks, write down your answers to the questions, important page numbers, and any other ideas you would like to discuss with your group.

FICTION

1. Do the characters in your book act like real people? What makes them seem real or not real?

2. What is the setting of your book? How does the author give you information about it?

3. How does the author use action, dialogue, thoughts, or descriptions to create a mood or affect your emotions?

FICTION

1. What do you think might happen next? What clues has the author given you?

2. What is the most important idea in this section? Why?

3. What did you like the most about what you just read? What did you like the least? Why?

NONFICTION

1. How does the author organize the information? How does this organization help you understand the text?

2. What main idea or ideas is the author writing about?

3. Is the information enjoyable to read? How does the author get and keep your attention?

NONFICTION

1. What opinions, if any, does the author express?

2. What kinds of graphic aids does the author include? How do they help you understand the text?

3. After reading this section, what are some things you would like to learn more about?

～Literature Circle Bookmarks～

Notes

_____
_____
_____

Notes

_____
_____
_____

Notes

_____
_____
_____

Notes

_____
_____
_____

© Harcourt

Literature Circle Roles

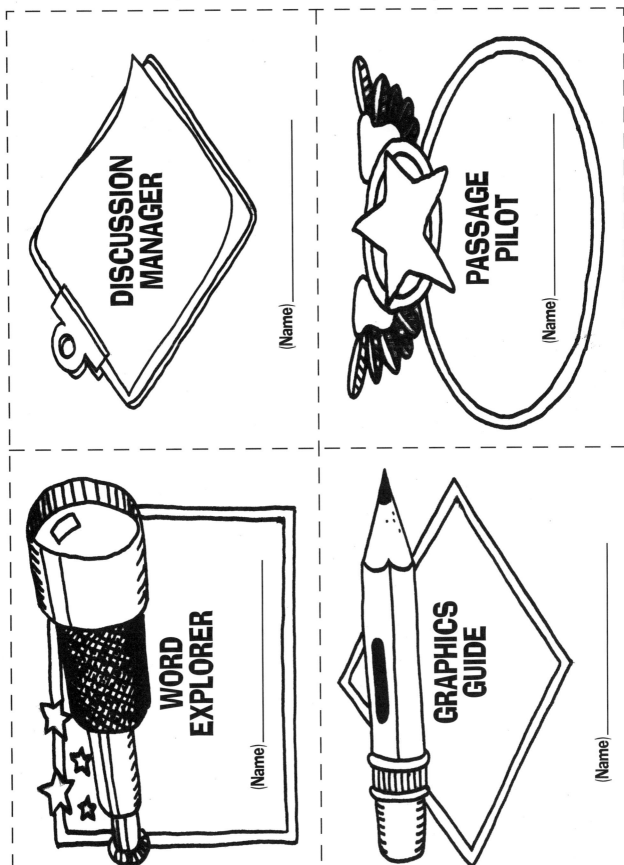

DISCUSSION MANAGER

(Name) _____

PASSAGE PILOT

(Name) _____

WORD EXPLORER

(Name) _____

GRAPHICS GUIDE

(Name) _____

© Harcourt

Literature Circle Roles

PASSAGE PILOT

- Find parts of the text that you think are important or interesting enough to share.
- Plan to read these parts aloud or to have others do so.

DISCUSSION MANAGER

- Make a list of questions to open the discussion.
- Ask about important ideas and about readers' thoughts.
- Involve each member in the discussion.

GRAPHICS GUIDE

- Draw and share a sketch, diagram, or other graphic that shows something about the book or an idea, thought, or feeling you had while reading.
- Explain your graphic.

WORD EXPLORER

- As you read, watch for important or interesting words to point out to your group.
- Help your group members find these words and discuss their meanings.
- Find out meanings of words you don't know.

© Harcourt

Literature Circle Roles

SHARING SUPERVISOR

(Name)

SUMMARY STARTER

(Name)

FACT FINDER

(Name)

SETTINGS NAVIGATOR

(Name)

Literature Circle Roles

SUMMARY STARTER

- Write a short statement to sum up what you read.
- For fiction, tell the most important events of the story.
- For nonfiction, tell the main idea or ideas.
- Lead the group in identifying a one-sentence summary of the text.

SHARING SUPERVISOR

- Lead the group in deciding on a creative way to share what you read.
- Gather the supplies your group needs.
- Make sure the group is ready to present to the class.

SETTINGS NAVIGATOR

- Keep track of the times and places, or settings, mentioned in your book.
- Create a map or diagram to show how the setting changes.

FACT FINDER

- Choose something you read about that either interests or puzzles you.
- Use reference sources to find a piece of information to share about that topic.
- Find information about ideas your group wants to explore further.

～Literature Circle ✓ Checklist ～

Fill out this checklist after each meeting of your Literature Circle. Check **Yes** or **No** for each item. Then write at the bottom what you would like to do better next time. Look at the checklist again before the next meeting of your Literature Circle.

NAME _____ **DATE** _____

TITLE _____ **AUTHOR** _____

▶ WAS I READY FOR LITERATURE CIRCLE?

	Yes	No
Did I bring my book?		
Did I do the reading we agreed upon?		
Did I either write notes for my role or write in my journal?		

▶ DID I TAKE PART IN THE DISCUSSION?

	Yes	No
Did I share my ideas and feelings?		
Did I ask questions about things I didn't understand?		
Did I listen carefully to others?		

▶ WHAT CAN I DO BETTER NEXT TIME?

_____

_____

_____

_____

_____

_____

Learning Contracts

A learning contract is a written agreement between a student and teacher that sets conditions for independent study. For example, the contract may specify tasks that the student is to complete, terms that the student must abide by, and a date by which the contract is to be completed. Learning contracts give students a taste of independence balanced by a sense of taking responsibility for their own work.

A BALANCED APPROACH

INDEPENDENCE
- work at own pace
- make decisions

RESPONSIBILITY
- observe terms of contract
- complete task on time

LEARNING CONTRACTS

Learning Contracts for Independent Reading

You can use contracts to encourage above-level readers to read more difficult books at their own pace and to share their responses in innovative ways. Keep in mind that even good readers may need some guidance to learn to pace themselves appropriately. To help develop pacing skills, you may want to establish checkpoints at which you review the student's progress, as well as end dates by which the reading and the student's response to the literature should be completed.

A copying master for an independent reading contract can be found on page 153. You can also adapt this contract to use for other types of independent projects.

INDEPENDENT READING CONTRACT

1. I will read this book: _____

(title)

by _____

(author)

2. I will complete the book by this date: _____

3. I will respond to the literature and share it with classmates in the following way:

_____

_____

_____

_____

4. I will complete my response or sharing by this date: _____

5. I agree to work within the following guidelines:

_____

_____

_____

_____

6. I agree to checkpoints that my teacher may list on a separate sheet of paper and attach to this contract.

Student and teacher agree to all of the terms stated in this contract.

DATE OF SIGNING: _____

SIGNATURE OF STUDENT _____

SIGNATURE OF TEACHER _____

Writing Rubrics

The rubrics on the following pages give criteria for evaluating students' writing. As you analyze your students' written work and talk to students about their writing, you will want to emphasize the Traits of Good Writing shown in this diagram.

The Traits of Good Writing

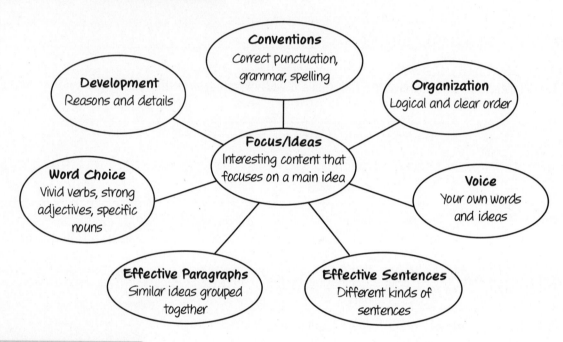

Conventions
Correct punctuation, grammar, spelling

Development
Reasons and details

Organization
Logical and clear order

Focus/Ideas
Interesting content that focuses on a main idea

Word Choice
Vivid verbs, strong adjectives, specific nouns

Voice
Your own words and ideas

Effective Paragraphs
Similar ideas grouped together

Effective Sentences
Different kinds of sentences

Using the Rubrics

FOR ASSESSMENT Use the rubrics to score a student's work by noting which criteria best describe the piece of writing you are evaluating. Students can also use the rubrics to assess their own writing or for peer assessment in pairs or small groups. You may want to have students attach the marked rubric to the piece of writing in their portfolios so they can assess their progress over the course of the school year. You may also use the rubrics to point out strengths and areas for improvement in conferences with students and their family members.

AS TEACHING TOOLS Before students begin each writing assignment, discuss with them the rubric for the type of writing they are about to do. Have them set goals for their writing by focusing on the criteria for excellence, and encourage them to suggest other important criteria to add to the rubric. Then, as students work through the stages of the writing process, have them refer to appropriate points in the rubric to remind them what to include or how to improve their writing.

© Harcourt

Four-Point Scoring Rubric

	Score of 4 ★★★★	Score of 3 ★★★	Score of 2 ★★	Score of 1 ★
Focus/Ideas	The paper is completely focused on the task and has a clear purpose.	The paper is generally focused on the task and the purpose.	The paper is somewhat focused on the task and purpose.	The paper does not have a clear focus or a purpose.
Organization/ Paragraphs	The paper has a clear beginning, middle, and ending. The ideas and details are presented in logical order. The writer uses transitions, such as *Finally, The next day*, or *However*, to show the relationships among ideas.	The ideas and details are mostly presented in logical order. The writer uses some transitions to show the relationships among ideas.	The organization is not clear in some places.	The paper has little or no organization.
Development	The paper has a clear central idea that is supported by strong, specific details.	The paper has a central idea and is supported by details.	The paper does not have a clear central idea and has few supporting details.	The central idea is not clear and there are few or no supporting details.
Voice	The writer's viewpoint is clear. The writer uses creative and original phrases and expressions where appropriate.	The writer's viewpoint is somewhat clear. The writer uses some original phrases and expressions.	The writer's viewpoint is unclear.	The writer seems uninterested in what he or she is writing about.
Word Choice	The writer uses clear, exact words and phrases. The writing is interesting to read.	The word choices are clear. The writer uses some interesting words and phrases.	The writer does not use words or phrases that make the writing clear to the reader.	The writer uses word choices that are unclear or inappropriate.
Sentences	The writer uses a variety of sentences. The writing flows smoothly.	The writer uses some variety in sentences.	The writer does not use much variety in his or her sentences.	There is little or no variety in sentences. Some of the sentences are unclear.
Conventions	There are few or no errors in grammar, punctuation, capitalization, and spelling.	There are few errors in grammar, punctuation, capitalization, and spelling.	There are some errors in grammar, punctuation, capitalization, and spelling.	There are many errors in grammar, punctuation, capitalization, and spelling.

Six-Point Scoring Rubric

	Score of 6 ★★★★★★	Score of 5 ★★★★★	Score of 4 ★★★★	Score of 3 ★★★	Score of 2 ★★	Score of 1 ★
Focus	The writing is completely focused on the topic and has a clear purpose.	The writing is focused on the topic and purpose.	The writing is generally focused on the topic and purpose.	The writing is somewhat focused on the topic and purpose.	The writing is related to the topic but does not have a clear focus.	The writing is not focused on the topic and purpose.
Organization	The ideas in the paper are well-organized and presented in logical order. The paper seems complete to the reader.	The organization of the paper is mostly clear. The paper seems complete.	The organization is mostly clear, but the paper may seem unfinished.	The paper is somewhat organized, but seems unfinished.	There is little organization to the paper.	There is no organization to the paper.
Support	The writing has strong, specific details. The word choices are clear and fresh.	The writing has strong, specific details and clear word choices.	The writing has supporting details and some variety in word choice.	The writing has few supporting details. It needs more variety in word choice.	The writing uses few supporting details and very little variety in word choice.	There are few or no supporting details. The word choices are unclear.
Conventions	The writer uses a variety of sentences. There are few or no errors in grammar, spelling, punctuation, and capitalization.	The writer uses a variety of sentences. There are few errors in grammar, spelling, punctuation, and capitalization.	The writer uses some variety in sentences. There are a few errors in grammar, spelling, punctuation, and capitalization.	The writer uses simple sentences. There are some errors in grammar, spelling, punctuation, and capitalization.	The writer uses simple sentences. There are many errors in grammar, spelling, punctuation, and capitalization.	The writer uses unclear sentences. There are many errors in grammar, spelling, punctuation, and capitalization.

Presentation Scoring Rubric

	Score of 6 ★★★★★★	Score of 5 ★★★★★	Score of 4 ★★★★	Score of 3 ★★★	Score of 2 ★★	Score of 1 ★
Handwriting	The slant of the letters is the same throughout the whole paper. The letters are clearly formed and the spacing between words is equal, which makes the text very easy to read.	The slant of the letters is almost the same through most of the paper. The letters are clearly formed. The spacing between words is usually equal.	The slant of the letters is usually the same. The letters are clearly formed most of the time. The spacing between words is usually equal.	The handwriting is readable. There are some differences in letter shape and form, slant, and spacing that make some words easier to read than others.	The handwriting is somewhat readable. There are many differences in letter shape and form, slant, and spacing that make some words hard to read.	The letters are not formed correctly. The slant spacing is not the same throughout the paper, or there is no regular space between words. The paper is very difficult to read.
Word Processing	Fonts and sizes are used very well, which helps the reader enjoy reading the text.	Fonts and sizes are used well.	Fonts and sizes are used fairly well, but could be improved upon.	Fonts and sizes are used well in some places, but make the paper look cluttered in others.	Fonts and sizes are not used well. The paper looks cluttered.	The writer has used too many different fonts and sizes. It is very distracting to the reader.
Markers	The title, side heads, page numbers, and bullets are used very well. They make it easy for the reader to find information in the text. These markers clearly show how the writer organized the information.	The title, side heads, page numbers, and bullets are used well. They help the reader find information.	The title, side heads, page numbers, and bullets are used fairly well. They usually help the reader find information.	The writer uses some markers such as a title, page numbers, or bullets. However, the use of markers could be improved upon to help the reader to get more meaning from the text.	The writer uses very few markers. This makes it hard for the reader to find and understand the information in the text.	There are no markers such as a title, page numbers, bullets, or side heads.
Visuals	The writer uses visuals such as illustrations, charts, graphs, maps, and tables very well. The text and visuals clearly relate to each other.	The writer uses visuals well. The text and visuals relate to each other.	The writer uses visuals fairly well.	The writer uses visuals with the text, but the reader may not understand how they are related.	The writer tries to use visuals with the text, but the reader is confused by them.	The visuals do not make sense with the text.
Speaking	The speaker uses very effective pacing, volume, intonation, and expression.	The speaker uses effective pacing, volume, intonation, and expression.	The speaker uses mostly effective pacing, volume, intonation, and expression.	The speaker uses somewhat effective pacing, volume, intonation, and expression.	The speaker needs to work on pacing, volume, intonation, and expression.	The speaker's techniques are unclear or distracting to the listener.

Vocabulary Activities

These activities can be used to practice specific vocabulary words from the lesson plans for the Library Books or to extend and enrich your students' vocabularies. Mix and match activities according to your needs.

▶ Vocabulary Password

Team A	Team B
⊬⊬⊬⊬	|||

MATERIALS:

• word cards with a vocabulary word on each card
• paper and pencils for keeping score

DIRECTIONS:

1. This game can be played by two teams of two to four players, plus one additional student who acts as Quiz Master.
2. The Quiz Master gives a word card to a player on Team A. The player defines the word without using the word itself. If the other players on Team A guess the word and use it in a sentence, their team gets one point.
3. If Team A cannot guess the word, the Quiz Master gives the same card to a player on Team B. That player gives his or her team a different clue for the word. If Team B guesses correctly and uses the word in a sentence, they get one point. If not, Team A gets another turn, and so on.
4. When the first word is guessed correctly, the Quiz Master begins the second round by giving Team B a new word. Teams continue to take turns, starting each round with a new word.

▶ In a Spin

MATERIALS:

• simple cardboard spinner, as shown

DIRECTIONS:

1. Divide the spinner into sections, and write a vocabulary word in each section.
2. Two to four players take turns spinning the pointer.
3. The player who spins reads aloud the word on which the arrow stops. He or she then gives a definition for the word and uses it in a sentence.

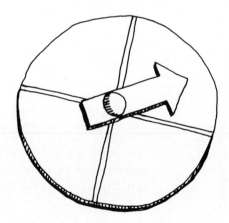

Vocabulary Activities

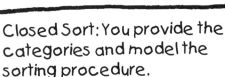

▶ The Word Bug

MATERIALS:
- slips of paper with vocabulary words
- paper bag or small box
- picture of "Word Bug"
- chalkboard, chalk

DIRECTIONS:
1. Divide students into two teams. Fold the slips of paper with the vocabulary words, and place them in a paper bag or small box. Designate a small area on the chalkboard for each team.
2. The first player on Team A draws a slip of paper from the bag or box, reads the word aloud, and gives its definition. If the definition is correct, the player draws one part of the Word Bug's body on the chalkboard. If the definition is not correct, another team member can provide the correct definition but does not draw a part of the bug's body.
3. The two teams take turns picking words until one team has completed its drawing of the Word Bug.

VARIATION: This game can also be played by pairs of students. Player A picks a slip of paper and reads the word aloud. Player B gives the definition. If the definition is correct, Player B draws one part of the Word Bug. Players take turns until one of them has drawn the complete bug.

▶ Sort Them Out

MATERIALS:
- paper
- pencils

DIRECTIONS:
1. Have students work in pairs or small groups to sort vocabulary words into categories. Categories might be based on similarities or differences in letter or syllable patterns, word meanings, parts of speech, or ways words are used. You may want to extend the activity by having students think of similar words to add to the completed categories.
2. After students have completed their sorts, have them compare and discuss their work with other pairs or groups.
3. Depending on the words you are using, the skill level of your students, and students' familiarity with word sorts, you might choose any of the options listed.

> **Closed Sort:** You provide the categories and model the sorting procedure.
>
> **Blind Sort:** You provide the categories. Students work in pairs. One calls out a word; the other indicates where it belongs.
>
> **Writing Sort:** You provide the categories and call out the words. Students write the words in the appropriate categories.
>
> **Open Sort:** Students create categories based on the words to be sorted.

© Harcourt

Vocabulary Activities

▶ Tell a Story

MATERIALS:
- writing paper
- pencils
- tape recorder
- audiocassette tape

DIRECTIONS:
1. Have students work in small groups to make up brief stories or dialogues that include vocabulary words.
2. Depending on the available words and students' abilities, you may want to assign particular vocabulary words or set a minimum number of vocabulary words that students must use.
3. Students can write their stories or dialogues on paper and then record them. Have students play their tapes for classmates, who listen for the vocabulary words and decide whether they are used correctly.

▶ Across and Down

MATERIALS:
- scrap paper
- pencils
- graph paper

DIRECTIONS:
1. Students work in pairs or small groups to construct puzzles using vocabulary words. Suggest that students look for shared letters and try different combinations on scrap paper until the puzzle looks good to them.
2. Have students copy their completed puzzle on graph paper and number each word in the puzzle.
3. Tell students to write clues for each of the words in the puzzle. A clue might be in the form of a picture, a definition, an antonym, or a sentence with a blank for the target word.
4. Have students exchange and complete each other's puzzles.

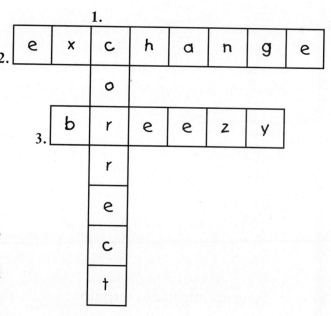

DOWN
1. not wrong

ACROSS
2. trade
3. A light wind blows on a _____ day.

Vocabulary Activities

▶ What's My Word?

MATERIALS:

- cards with vocabulary words
- chalkboard, chalk

DIRECTIONS:

1. Mix the vocabulary cards and place them face down.
2. The first player takes the top card and reads the word silently. He or she can pantomime the word or illustrate it on the board but cannot speak or write.
3. The other students try to guess the word. If they cannot figure it out in several tries, the student with the card can choose a classmate to help him or her communicate the meaning of the vocabulary word.
4. After students have guessed the correct word, another student takes the next card on the pile, and play continues.

Burden

▶ Idiom Collecting

MATERIALS:

- chart paper
- markers

DIRECTIONS:

1. Choose one or more idiomatic expressions that students have come across in their reading. Write the idioms on chart paper, and ask students to illustrate them in both their figurative and literal senses.

Seeing Red

2. Use the expression to begin an idiom collection. Encourage students to add and illustrate idioms they encounter in their reading or other media or in their everyday lives.
3. As the collection grows, suggest that students look for ways to categorize the idioms. For example, some expressions refer to colors ("green with envy," "feeling blue"); some mention foods ("take the cake," "butter someone up"), and so on. Students might also categorize idioms that use a particular word ("get cold feet," "give the cold shoulder to," "throw cold water on.")

Using Retelling to Assess Comprehension

▶ Retelling

Retelling is an assessment strategy that may be used to measure a student's strengths and weaknesses in comprehension. Listening to a retelling provides insights into a student's ability to construct meaning, to identify important information, to make inferences, and to organize and summarize information. Specifically, listening to a retelling can help you assess whether the student

- relates the main idea and relevant details in sequence
- provides a summarizing statement
- includes story elements
- uses phrases, language, or vocabulary from the text
- evaluates an author's point of view, purpose, or craft
- stays on topic
- understands relationships in the text
- provides extensions of the text
- relates text to relevant experiences

▶ Oral Retelling

When conducting an oral retelling, ask students to tell the story in their own words. Try not to interrupt. Allow plenty of time for a student to complete an oral retelling, and be sure the student has nothing more to say before ending the session.

For the emerging reader who is reading books with limited text, the retelling may be short and fairly simple: adjust criteria in the attached rubric as necessary. For more complex books, if a student needs prompting, try using generic statements such as "Tell me more," "Keep going," and "You're doing a good job." If you need to elicit more information, prompt the student by asking open-ended questions such as these:

- What was the character's main problem?
- What was your favorite part of the story?
- Where did the story take place?
- Who else was in the story?
- How did the story end?
- What else do you remember from the story?

▶ Written Retelling

When conducting a written retelling, ask students to tell the story in their own words and not to worry about spelling or handwriting. Allow plenty of time for students to finish writing before ending the session.

Use the rubric on the following page to assess oral and written retellings.

© Harcourt

～Scoring Rubric for Retellings～

SCORE	CHARACTERISTICS
3	**Proficient: Student retells the text using complex responses that demonstrate a thorough understanding and interpretation of the text.** • relates the main idea and important and supporting details • relates text in sequence • provides a summarizing statement • includes story elements such as setting, characters, plot, problems, and resolutions • uses phrases, language, vocabulary, sentence structure, or literary devices from the text • evaluates the author's point of view, purpose, or craft • stays on topic • discriminates between reality and fantasy, fact and fiction • understands relationships in text such as cause and effect • classifies, groups, compares, or contrasts information • provides extensions of the text by making connections to other texts, relating relevant experiences, or making generalizations
2	**Satisfactory: Student adequately retells the text and demonstrates an understanding of the text.** • relates the main idea and relevant details • relates most of the text in sequence • includes story elements such as setting, characters, main problem, and resolution • uses language or vocabulary from the text • stays on topic • discriminates between reality and fantasy • understands relationships in text such as cause and effect • classifies, groups, compares, or contrasts information • provides some extensions of the text by making connections to other texts or relating relevant experiences
1	**Minimal: Student makes several inaccurate, incomplete, or irrelevant statements or otherwise provides evidence of lack of comprehension.** • misunderstands main idea and omits important details • relates text out of sequence • omits story elements or provides incorrect information about setting, characters, and plot • provides a poorly organized or unclear structure • provides no extensions of the text

～Individual Reading Inventory～

The three Library Books on the following pages are accompanied by a two-page Individual Reading Inventory (IRI) feature in addition to their regular lessons. These IRI features appear on pages 166–171.

What Is an IRI?

An Individual Reading Inventory is an assessment tool for learning about a student's reading strategies and for planning instruction. While a student is reading aloud, the teacher records everything he or she says or does. An IRI has two primary parts: a reading passage and comprehension questions.

Administering the IRI

1. Before the reading, explain the task. Tell the student that he or she will read a passage aloud and then answer four questions.
2. During the reading, unobtrusively record oral miscues on the Individual Reading Inventory Form. Use the Marking Oral Reading Miscues chart to record oral errors and self-corrections.
3. After the reading, ask the student the questions at the bottom of the Individual Reading Inventory Form. Mark correct (+) and incorrect (-) responses.

Miscues

Total the number of miscues and self-corrections. Then follow the steps on the Individual Reading Inventory Summary Form to compute the Error Rate. Look for an Error Rate of 10% or less to confirm instructional reading level and 5% or less to confirm independent reading level.

Error Rate

1. Total the number of miscues.
2. Subtract the total number of self-corrections from the total number of miscues for a subtotal.
3. Divide this subtotal by the word count of the passage.

Fluency

Count the number of words read correctly in one minute. Count repetitions and self-corrections as correctly read words. Look for the following ranges of correctly read words per minute:

- 40–60 by the end of grade one
- 60–90 by the end of grade two
- 110–120 by the end of grade three
- 115–125 by the end of grade four
- 125–135 by the end of grade five
- 130–150 by the end of grade six

Comprehension

Total the number of correct responses to the questions. Look for a score of 75% or higher to confirm instructional reading level. To help evaluate comprehension errors, questions 1 and 2 require literal thinking, and questions 3 and 4 require inferential thinking.

Marking Oral Reading Miscues

READING MISCUE	MARKING	SAMPLE
1. Omissions	Circle the word, word part, or phrase omitted.	I will let you (go) in.
2. Insertions	Insert a caret (∧) and write in the inserted word or phrase.	We bought a ∧big parrot.
3. Substitutions	Write the word or phrase the student substitutes above the word or phrase in the text.	Dad fixed ~~my~~ the bike.
4. Mispronunciations	Write the phonetic mispronunciation above the word.	Have you ~~fed~~ feed the dog?
5. Self-corrections	Write the letters SC next to the miscue that is self-corrected.	We took our space. SC
6. Repetitions	Draw a line under any part of the text that is repeated.	It is your garden garden now.
7. Punctuation	Circle punctuation missed. Write in any punctuation inserted.	Take them home . Then come back and you and I will go to town.
8. Hesitations	Place vertical lines at places where the student hesitates excessively.	Pretend / this is mine.

Individual Reading Inventory Form

STUDENT: _____   DATE: _____

SELECTION TITLE: *And Then What Happened, Paul Revere?*,   WORD COUNT: 127
pages 8–10

And there was plenty for Paul to do. When he was fifteen years old, his father died, and Paul took over the silversmithing business. He made beads, rings, lockets, bracelets, buttons, medals, pitchers, teapots, spoons, sugar baskets, cups, ewers, porringers, shoe buckles, and candlesticks.

Once he made a silver collar for a man's pet squirrel.

To make extra money, he took a job ringing the bells in Christ Church. In Boston, church bells were rung not just on Sundays but three times a day on weekdays, at special hours on holidays and anniversaries, for fires and emergencies, whenever a member of the congregation died, and whenever there was especially good news or especially bad news to announce.

Comments: _____

_____

_____

_____

_____

Indicate correct (+) or incorrect (–) response for each question:

1. **How old was Paul when he took over his father's silversmithing business?** (fifteen years old)
2. **Name some of the objects Paul made.** (beads, rings, lockets, bracelets)
3. **What did Paul do to make extra money?** (He took a job ringing the bells in church.)
4. **List one reason why church bells in Boston would ring three times a day on weekdays.** (whenever there was especially good news or especially bad news to announce)

Individual Reading Inventory Summary Form

STUDENT: _____   GRADE: _____   DATE: _____

PASSAGE: _____   WORD COUNT: _____

1. Miscues

Total number of miscues _____

    Meaning-based miscues _____

    Graphic/sound-based miscues _____

Comments and patterns observed: _____

_____

Total number of self-corrections _____

Comments and patterns observed: _____

_____

Error Rate

- Subtract the number of self-corrections from the total number of miscues for a subtotal.

- Divide the subtotal by the word count of the passage.

_____ ÷ _____ = _____

   (SUBTOTAL)   **(WORD COUNT)**   **ERROR RATE**

2. Fluency

Number of words read per minute _____

_____ ÷ _____ = _____

(NUMBER OF CORRECT   **(WORD COUNT)**   **FLUENCY RATE**
WORDS READ PER MINUTE)

Comments and patterns observed: _____

_____

3. Comprehension

_____ ÷ 4 x 100 = _____%

(TOTAL CORRECT ANSWERS)   **COMPREHENSION SCORE**

Comments and patterns observed: _____

_____

Summary Comments

_____

Individual Reading Inventory Form

STUDENT: _____   **DATE:** _____

SELECTION TITLE: *Stone Wall Secrets*, page 6   **WORD COUNT: 125**

    The autumn weather was warm, the ground firm and dry. It was the perfect time to tour the old farm and patch any walls needing repair—a chore that Grampa had always loved to do. Usually only a stone or two would slip to one side, jostled by frost or the roots of a tree. But once in a while, a short stretch of wall would collapse and need to be rebuilt.

    Grampa and Adam followed a well-worn path through ghosts of pastures now thick with pine. They hiked first through the small orchard, loading their pockets with fruit plucked from gnarled limbs. But along each wall, they slowed their pace, stopping now and then to return a fallen stone to its rightful place.

Comments: _____

_____

_____

_____

_____

Indicate correct (+) or incorrect (–) response for each question:

1. **What chore did Grampa love to do?** (tour the old farm and patch any walls needing repair)
2. **Why would a stone slip to one side?** (It would be jostled by frost or the roots of a tree.)
3. **What would happen to the wall once in a while?** (It would collapse and need to be rebuilt.)
4. **What did Grampa and Adam load their pockets with?** (fruit plucked from the gnarled limbs of trees in the small orchard)

© Harcourt

Individual Reading Inventory Summary Form

STUDENT: _____   GRADE: _____   DATE: _____

PASSAGE: _____   WORD COUNT: _____

1. Miscues

Total number of miscues _____

    Meaning-based miscues _____

    Graphic/sound-based miscues _____

Comments and patterns observed: _____

_____

Total number of self-corrections _____

Comments and patterns observed: _____

_____

Error Rate

- Subtract the number of self-corrections from the total number of miscues for a subtotal.

- Divide the subtotal by the word count of the passage.

_____ ÷ _____ = _____

   (SUBTOTAL)   (WORD COUNT)   ERROR RATE

2. Fluency

Number of words read per minute _____

_____ ÷ _____ = _____

(NUMBER OF CORRECT   (WORD COUNT)   FLUENCY RATE
WORDS READ PER MINUTE)

Comments and patterns observed: _____

_____

3. Comprehension

_____ ÷ 4 x 100 = _____%

(TOTAL CORRECT ANSWERS)   COMPREHENSION SCORE

Comments and patterns observed: _____

_____

Summary Comments

_____

Individual Reading Inventory Form

STUDENT: _____ **DATE:** _____

SELECTION TITLE: *Beetles, Lightly Toasted,* pages 114–115 **WORD COUNT: 111**

There were footsteps in the hall, then the principal came in, followed by a gray-haired man in a blue suit. His eyes seemed to take in the whole room at once, and he smiled as the principal introduced him. Then he sat down on the edge of Mrs. Haynes' desk and looked the students over.

"I was disappointed," he said, "that only nine of you decided to enter my contest this year, but I'm delighted with those who did. It just goes to show that imagination is alive and well in these United States, and if the future of our country depends on people like you, then we're in good hands."

Comments: _____

_____

_____

_____

_____

_____

Indicate correct (+) or incorrect (–) response for each question:

1. **Who introduces the man in the blue suit to the class?** (the principal)
2. **How many students entered the contest?** (nine)
3. **Why is the man delighted with the students who entered the contest?** (They showed imagination.)
4. **Why does the man say that the contestants make him feel that the future of the United States is in good hands?** (He feels that creative and imaginative people are important to the future of the country.)

© Harcourt

Individual Reading Inventory Summary Form

STUDENT: _____   GRADE: _____   DATE: _____

PASSAGE: _____   WORD COUNT: _____

1. Miscues

Total number of miscues _____

  Meaning-based miscues _____

  Graphic/sound-based miscues _____

Comments and patterns observed: _____

_____

Total number of self-corrections _____

Comments and patterns observed: _____

_____

Error Rate

- Subtract the number of self-corrections from the total number of miscues for a subtotal.

- Divide the subtotal by the word count of the passage.

_____ ÷ _____ = _____

   (SUBTOTAL)   (WORD COUNT)   ERROR RATE

2. Fluency

Number of words read per minute _____

_____ ÷ _____ = _____

(NUMBER OF CORRECT   (WORD COUNT)   FLUENCY RATE

WORDS READ PER MINUTE)

Comments and patterns observed: _____

_____

3. Comprehension

_____ ÷ 4 x 100 = _____%

(TOTAL CORRECT ANSWERS)   COMPREHENSION SCORE

Comments and patterns observed: _____

_____

Summary Comments

_____

The Black Stallion

Page 18
1. excited, thrilled, admiring, astonished
2. Alec grabs a rope attached to the stallion and ties it around his waist. The stallion pulls Alec to shore.
3. He uses the pocketknife to cut the rope attaching him to the stallion.

Page 19
1. He builds a shelter and finds food; he recalls that a kind of seaweed can be eaten.
2. He mounts the stallion and is thrown off; gradually the stallion lets him ride.
3. the smoke from the fire

Page 20
1. Possible responses: Alec's story sounds unbelievable; he might not be thinking clearly.
2. Alec swims underwater to put a band around the stallion, who is then hoisted up to the ship.
3. gentle when Alec is nearby; wild and fierce when he is not

Page 21
1. The stallion refuses to come down the gangplank; Alec blindfolds him.
2. Henry owns the barn where the stallion will be stabled. Tony is a vegetable seller who keeps his horse Napoleon there. Joe Russo is a reporter.
3. Responses will vary.

Page 22
1. This would help Henry recall his glorious past as a jockey and trainer.
2. To race, the stallion must be registered. They need to know the stallion's parentage to do this, and they do not have the information.
3. Responses will vary.

Page 23
1. Because Napoleon is old, he does not threaten the stallion.
2. Only registered horses are allowed, and Henry does not want the horse distracted.
3. Responses will vary.

Page 24
1. As the horse has no registration papers, he cannot run in a regular race.
2. He gets the stallion included in a special race.
3. He is determined and confident about the race.

Page 25
1. Responses will vary.
2. Responses will vary.
3. Responses will vary.

Page 29
1. C 2. F 3. C 4. G 5. D 6. G 7. C 8. G 9. C
10. Students should relate their answers to specific events in the story as they explain whether or not

anyone besides Alec will ever be able to ride the stallion.

Sees Behind Trees

Page 32
1. He is sure he will fail the shooting test.
2. Possible response: She makes him use other senses instead of his eyes.
3. The weroance knew that Walnut could not pass the shooting test.

Page 33
1. Possible response: It is the same in most ways, but people treat him with more respect.
2. Possible response: He is honored to be the first to hear it.
3. Possible response: He feels as if a part of himself was left behind.

Page 34
1. He says he will fast until Sees Behind Trees returns.
2. He tells Sees Behind Trees to let his body show him the way.
3. Possible response: No one else lives close by.

Page 35
1. Responses will vary.
2. Possible responses: learning about yourself; learning to be alone
3. Responses will vary.

Page 39
1. C 2. G 3. A 4. G 5. D 6. F 7. C 8. H 9. D
10. Responses will vary. Responses might describe the qualities Sees Behind Trees has gained from his journey, including patience, wisdom, and courage.

Baseball in the Barrios

Page 42
1. He's a good student and close to his family, but he'd rather play baseball than do anything else in the world.
2. It is played in both North and South America.
3. There was prejudice against Latin Americans then, and language and transportation were problems as well.

Page 43
1. He began playing organized baseball when he was four.
2. Like him, they are from Venezuela and played shortstop. They were also his father's favorite players.
3. They go to all his games; his father helps him practice and teaches him about the game.

Page 44
1. Pickup games might be played on the street, on basketball courts, or just about anywhere.
2. They play *chapitas*, a form of baseball in which they must hit tiny bottle caps.

3. Both fought to free their countries from European rule; Washington was North American, and Bolívar was South American.

Page 45
1. Responses may vary. Students should identify at least one character from another reading selection and discuss him or her in relation to Hubaldo.
2. Responses may vary. Possible themes include: achieving an important goal requires commitment, hard work, and support; and baseball is a sport popular in many countries in addition to the United States.
3. Responses may vary. Students should discuss one personal goal and show how it is similar to and different from Hubaldo's goal.

Page 49
1. C 2. G 3. C 4. J 5. A 6. G 7. A 8. H 9. D
10. Responses may vary. Students should include specific details from the book about Hubaldo's character, actions, and/or circumstances to support their answers.

The Tarantula in My Purse
Page 52
1. Possible response: She had grown up raising wild animals in the house and let her children do the same thing.
2. He liked to take showers and watch television.
3. The goose thought it was human, and the duck thought it was a goose.

Page 53
1. Possible response: She knew crows often try to get even with someone who hurts them.
2. Possible responses: New York knew the author wanted to catch him; Dr. Kalmbach's crow teased a neighbor's dog and got it to tear up the cabbages; crows can learn to talk.
3. Possible response: Luke meant that the crayfish could not be blamed for killing other animals.

Page 54
1. It was best to try to get the babies back to their mothers.
2. Luke believed animals should be returned to the wild as soon as possible. Twig and Craig would rather keep them as pets.
3. A flock of wild crows attracted Crowbar, and he left with them.

Page 55
1. Responses will vary.
2. Possible responses: They learned to respect nature; they learned that many animals have personalities.
3. Responses will vary.

Page 59
1. D 2. G 3. A 4. G 5. D 6. H 7. A 8. J 9. B
10. Responses will vary. Students should mention specific ideas. They may list positives, such as saving hurt or abandoned animals and learning about

nature, or they may list negatives, such as making animals dependent on humans and interfering with nature.

Maria's Comet
Page 62
1. She thought that he swept the sky with a broom, making the dust fly up into the sky to make stars. Now she knows that he observes the stars through his telescope.
2. The astronomer slowly scans across the sky with a telescope, observing the stars, in much the same way as a sailor slowly scans across the waves with a hand-held telescope, looking for boats and other objects.
3. The telescope gathers and focuses light to concentrate on the visible image, making its features more distinct.

Page 63
1. They are "mysterious" because at that time, scientists did not know what comets were made of. They are "visitors" because they streak across the sky briefly, unlike stars, which are constant.
2. Seven; because Maria does not mention Neptune and Pluto, readers can conclude that they have not yet been discovered.
3. Sad; she would rather be with him, looking through the telescope.

Page 64
1. They both want to be explorers. Andrew wants to explore the sea, and Maria wants to explore the nighttime sky.
2. Although she is sad that Andrew has gone away, she helps her family cope. She probably deals with conflicting emotions. She is sad because she misses Andrew. She is also glad that he is pursuing his goal.
3. She asks to go with him to the rooftop observatory. She is afraid he will say no because women in her time were supposed to learn home skills rather than develop scientific interests.

Page 65
1. a silvery patchwork of different patterns, created by the different stars, planets, and constellations
2. Even though he is far away, he can see the same stars; he is on a ship, and sailors use Polaris to help them determine their location.
3. Responses will vary.

Page 69
1. C 2. G 3. B 4. F 5. B 6. H 7. D 8. G 9. C
10. Responses will vary, but should be supported by reasons.

Stone Wall Secrets
Page 72
1. He is not sure what to do. It is a good offer, but he has fond memories of the walls from his youth. He also wants to do the right thing for his grandson, who will inherit the property.

© Harcourt

2. by taking Adam to different places on the farm, having him look closely at the rocks and feel them, and telling him stories
3. There was an ancient ocean where the farm is.

Page 73
1. Some rocks formed where ancient seas used to be and were lifted to become mountains; also, rocks from volcanic mountains are broken down by the sun, wind, and rain and are then carried down to the ocean.
2. Possible responses: to present the information through a story to a person about the same age as the reader; to make information about rocks more interesting
3. He asks questions, listens carefully, and finds rocks to ask questions about.

Page 74
1. Once there were Indian hunters in the forest. Then settlers turned the forest into farmland. Now the farm is a quiet homestead.
2. He has a sense of humor. He cares about Adam and wants him to experience a "family tradition."
3. They value the rocks. They think of the stone walls as telling stories. The walls are not just rocks; they are part of history.

Page 75
1. Responses will vary.
2. that rocks tell stories; that rocks are not worthless; that the past is interesting
3. Responses will vary.

Page 79
1. D 2. G 3. C 4. J 5. A 6. G 7. A 8. F 9. C
10. Responses will vary. Possible response: They will not be sold. This seems to be suggested by Adam's taking the letter from his grandfather and burying it in his pocket. Also, every detail in the story points to a value and importance in the stones that goes far beyond money.

The Young Artist
Page 82
1. He is impressed with Adrian's drawings.
2. Possible responses: On Adrian's first day in the studio, he says that he already knows how to draw; he already knows that he wants to use oil paints and to specialize in landscapes.
3. It is difficult for an artist to earn a living painting only landscapes.

Page 83
1. The narrator teaches him to paint realistically, and the chef wants Adrian to make him look better than he does in real life.
2. The narrator suggests that the chef might not pay unless he is satisfied, and it seems to Adrian that even his teacher wants him to paint a lie.
3. At first, he is happy because he thinks the king wants to buy one of his castle pictures. Then he starts to worry because he does not understand why the king wants him to bring his paints and brushes.

Page 84
1. He does not want to paint portraits, particularly a group portrait, and everyone wants him to paint what he considers "lies."
2. He had insisted that Adrian paint the chef's portrait, thus bringing him to the king's attention. To get Adrian out of this dangerous situation, he helps Adrian plan what to do.
3. Even though the painting is for the king, if Adrian paints it he will feel shame rather than honor, since the painting will be false and unrealistic.

Page 85
1. Responses will vary. Students should identify at least one character from another reading selection and discuss a difficult and courageous choice he or she makes.
2. Responses will vary. Possible responses: Do not compromise about the truth; being true to one's artistic vision is important and noble; honor and virtue are rewarded.
3. Responses will vary. Students should express an opinion and use prior knowledge and details from the story to support it.

Page 89
1. C 2. J 3. A 4. G 5. A 6. F 7. A 8. H 9. B
10. Responses will vary. Students should include specific details from the book about Adrian's character, actions, and/or life story to support their answers.

Dear Benjamin Banneker
Page 92
1. Possible response: The author wanted to give more facts about Banneker than she could fit in the story.
2. Most African Americans were slaves.
3. He was curious and intelligent.

Page 93
1. He was willing to work hard to accomplish his goals.
2. Possible response: Today people can get more accurate information from other sources.
3. Possible response: They thought a black man could not write an almanac.

Page 94
1. Possible response: He knew that many slaves could not read or were not allowed to have books.
2. He wanted to point out that owning slaves went against what Jefferson had written in the Declaration of Independence.
3. Possible response: He thought it would prove to Jefferson that black people had abilities equal to those of white people.

Page 95
1. Responses will vary.
2. Possible response: One man's actions can have an important effect on the world.
3. Responses will vary.

Page 99
1. D **2.** G **3.** D **4.** J **5.** C **6.** H **7.** A **8.** J **9.** A
10. Responses will vary. Responses may discuss Banneker's scientific and mathematic innovations or his antislavery efforts.

Frindle
Page 102
1. Possible responses: Nick is funny, curious, inventive, clever, smart; Mrs. Granger is stern, scary, tiny, serious.
2. Possible responses: She is wise to his "teacher-stopper" tricks; she wants him to learn by doing research.
3. Possible responses: She is a good teacher because she demands high-quality work; she is very serious; she helps students take an active role in learning.

Page 103
1. Possible response: Mrs. Granger says that people give meaning to words. Nick wants to test that theory himself.
2. Possible response: I wouldn't like staying after school, but it would be fun to help Nick.
3. Responses will vary.

Page 104
1. She writes an article in the local paper, which is then noticed by the local station whose story is then noticed by national television programs.
2. Noticing a hot new fad that might prove extremely profitable, he quickly becomes involved in manufacturing and marketing items related to the frindle.
3. Possible response: He does not want Nick to know that he is going to be rich, which he feels might hamper Nick's ambitious spirit.

Page 105
1. Possible responses: Some things that may look like troublemaking may have positive results; creative thinking is very valuable; school can be fun; teachers help students in many different ways.
2. Possible responses: It enables him to test an established theory; it makes him famous and rich; it enables him to honor his teacher and set up a scholarship to help other students.
3. Possible response: She was a clever, caring teacher who supported my learning all the time; she pretended to oppose me in order to spark my creativity.

Page 109
1. B **2.** H **3.** B **4.** J **5.** B **6.** J **7.** A **8.** J **9.** C
10. Responses will vary. Possible response: By fighting against the use of *frindle*, Mrs. Granger cleverly helped it develop into a "real" word. Her resistance made Nick and the other students even more determined to use the word.

Beetles, Lightly Toasted
Page 112
1. He is imaginative, creative, reliable, and hardworking.
2. excited, anxious, curious, impatient, enthusiastic

3. Andy eagerly anticipates the contest because his name and photograph will be published in the newspaper if he wins it. He wants to win so he will feel important.

Page 113
1. disappointed, bored, upset, annoyed
2. They hold a boycott so that Mr. Sudermann will be forced to give them a new topic.
3. Some students may say that the boycott will fail because Jack plans to break it. Others may believe that the boycott will succeed because Mr. Sudermann would probably rather change the topic than cancel this year's contest.

Page 114
1. Possible responses: because they are mad at him for breaking the boycott; because they think he is a sneak for working on an essay topic without telling anyone that he planned to enter
2. because he likes the food they serve there; because he wants to prevent Aunt Wanda from opening her own restaurant there; because he thinks Bucksville has few decent places to eat
3. yes, because he is "determined to enter the contest"; because he thinks Russ, Dora, and Jack will enter it; because he gets a terrific idea for a topic

Page 115
1. He decides to write about sources of food that people have not thought about before.
2. First, he writes a letter to Iowa State University to find out which bugs can be eaten safely. Next, he collects brown beetles, feeds them cornmeal, and freezes them. Then he peels off their wings and legs and chops the bodies into pieces. Finally, he toasts the beetles in the oven and adds them to brownie batter.
3. Yes. His subject is imaginative and closely relates to the essay topic, conservation.

Page 116
1. They all enjoy eating the brownies, and no one discovers Andy's secret ingredient—toasted beetles.
2. Possible response: I think he plans to write about saving energy while cooking because he tries to cook food in unusual ways.
3. Sam, Andy, and Lois have to catch a cow that has gotten loose and is wandering in the road.

Page 117
1. Both families have worries about earning a living. The Mollers live on a quiet farm, eat supper early, and go to sleep by nine o'clock. The Hollinses live in Bucksville in back of a restaurant and eat supper late after their customers leave.
2. Rather than putting toasted beetles in brownies, Andy deep-fries earthworms. Instead of classmates trying the fried worms, a health inspector and Sam's sister unknowingly eat them.
3. They stay overnight at each other's houses. Sam helps Andy with his secret food experiments. Andy discusses his feelings with Sam.

Page 118
1. He adds boiled, chopped mealworm grubs to two egg salad sandwiches. Jack eats one sandwich; Lois eats the other.
2. Insects are a cheap source of fat and protein; insects can be harvested without using additional land.
3. He realizes that if he does win he will have to explain how he tested his contest idea. He will have to admit that he tried out his unusual recipes on his classmates and relatives.

Page 119
1. Responses will vary.
2. the importance of honesty, the value of imagination, that how food tastes is more important than how it looks
3. Possible response: No. I think Andy is wrong to keep the ingredients a secret. He betrays the trust of his family and friends, and he risks making them sick because he does not know for sure that the insects are safe to eat.

Page 123
1. C 2. J 3. D 4. F 5. B 6. G 7. C 8. J 9. A
10. Luther Sudermann picks Andy and Jack because they write imaginative essays about conservation. Jack explains how to save energy by cooking in unusual ways. Andy tells how to save money and the food supply by using insects for food.

The Cat Who Escaped from Steerage
Page 126
1. Yonkel and Rifke dislike it intensely, but Chanah and her brother make the best of it.
2. noisy, crowded, dirty, dark, unsanitary
3. She and Yaacov search the ship to look for the cat. When they reach the third-class deck, they seek help from a Polish woman. The woman calls a steward to take them back to steerage.

Page 127
1. The passengers become restless and cranky because steerage is crowded, stuffy, gloomy, muggy, and wet.
2. Instead of cramped, dark quarters, passengers on the upper decks enjoy luxurious accommodations with marble floors and full-length mirrors. They also eat delicious food, listen to music, and play tennis.
3. They plan to steal water from the third-class supply room.

Page 128
1. to christen the new baby
2. They notice that Yaacov reacts to neither the loud clanging of a ship's bell nor the clapping of hands.
3. excited, nervous, overwhelmed, joyful, anxious

Page 129
1. Responses will vary.

2. The author's message is that many immigrants are brave, adventurous people who are willing to endure hardships and face challenges for the chance of a better life.
3. Responses will vary. Students may say that they would most dislike traveling in steerage because it is noisy, crowded, and dark. They would find it hard to spend two weeks on a ship without running water, fresh air, or sunlight.

Page 133
1. D 2. H 3. D 4. F 5. B 6. G 7. A 8. G 9. C
10. Responses will vary. Possible response: Babies born on a ship could be christened by the captain; most deaf or blind immigrants were sent back.

And Then What Happened, Paul Revere?
Page 136
1. Boston was a busy port city, with many people and all kinds of shops.
2. Church bells were used to announce important events and communicate news.
3. Revere was busy, adventurous, talented, and a bit forgetful.

Page 137
1. They wanted to show the English that the colonists would never pay a tax on tea.
2. Possible responses: He was a good, fast rider; he was clever and brave.
3. He spent less time working as a silversmith and more time working against the English.

Page 138
1. He had to warn the people that the English troops were coming; he had to inform John Hancock and Samuel Adams about the English troops.
2. He needed the dog to go back to get his spurs.
3. They did not want him to warn the colonists that their troops were marching.

Page 139
1. Responses will vary.
2. Yes; he knew he could be shot for riding to warn the colonists, but he went anyway.
3. He helped the colonists win the battles of Lexington and Concord; these battles were the start of the American Revolution.

Page 143
1. D 2. H 3. B 4. J 5. C 6. F 7. B 8. H 9. B
10. Responses will vary. Students should support their answers by citing details such as the act being a just response to an unfair tax or the colonists being unfair in throwing blame on the Indians.

© Harcourt